PUBLIC ENEMY

OLIVIER CHOINIÈRE

PUBLIC ENEMY

TRANSADAPTED BY BOBBY THEODORE

PLAYWRIGHTS CANADA PRESS
TORONTO

LIBRARY AND ARCHIVES CANADA CATALOGUING IN PUBLICATION
Title: Public enemy / by Olivier Choinière ; transadapted by Bobby Theodore.
Other titles: Ennemi public. English
Names: Choinière, Olivier, 1973- author. | Theodore, Bobby, translator.
Description: A play. | Translation of: Ennemi public.
Identifiers: Canadiana (print) 2022018626x | Canadiana (ebook) 20220186340
| ISBN 9780369103574 (softcover) | ISBN 9780369103598 (PDF)
| ISBN 9780369103581 (HTML)
Classification: LCC PS8555.H623 E513 2022 | DDC C842/.54—dc23

Playwrights Canada Press operates on land which is the ancestral home of the Anishinaabe Nations (Ojibwe / Chippewa, Odawa, Potawatomi, Algonquin, Saulteaux, Nipissing, and Mississauga), the Wendat, and the members of the Haudenosaunee Confederacy (Mohawk, Oneida, Onondaga, Cayuga, Seneca, and Tuscarora), as well as Metis and Inuit peoples. It always was and always will be Indigenous land.

We acknowledge the financial support of the Canada Council for the Arts, the Ontario Arts Council (OAC), Ontario Creates, and the Government of Canada for our publishing activities.

Canada Council for the Arts | Conseil des arts du Canada
ONTARIO ARTS COUNCIL
CONSEIL DES ARTS DE L'ONTARIO
an Ontario government agency
un organisme du gouvernement de l'Ontario

Canada
ONTARIO CREATES | ONTARIO CRÉATIF

Ennemi public was first produced by le Centre du Théâtre d'Aujourd'hui and L'ACTIVITÉ at Théâtre d'Aujourd'hui, Montréal, from February 24 to March 21, 2015, with the following cast and creative team:

Cast: Frédéric Blanchette, Muriel Dutil, Amélie Grenier, Brigitte Lafleur, Steve Laplante, Alexane Jamieson, Alexis Plante

Director: Olivier Choinière
Assistant Director and Stage Manager: Stéphanie Capistran-Lalonde
Dramaturg: Jean Marc Dalpé
Set Design: Jean Bard
Costume Design: Elen Ewing
Lighting Design: Mathieu Marcil
Sound Design: Éric Forget
Props Design Angela Rassenti
Puppet Coach: Olivier Ducas
Video Design: Michel-Antoine Castonguay
Makeup and Hair: Sylvie Rolland-Provost
Technical Co-Directors: Jean-Philippe Charbonneau and Francis Laporte
Stagehand: Eric-William Quinn

CHARACTERS

ELIZABETH: Seventy-five-year-old woman; mother of James, Daniel, and Melissa.
JAMES: Man in his forties; Tyler's father.
DANIEL: Man in his early forties.
MELISSA: Woman in her late thirties; Olivia's mother.
SUZIE: Woman in her forties; Daniel's girlfriend in Act 3.
TYLER: A teenager, around fifteen years old.
OLIVIA: An eleven-year-old girl.
SQUIRREL: A black, grey, or white rodent.

SETTING

Elizabeth's open-concept apartment. Its contemporary design clashes with a few older or tatty pieces of furniture. The action plays out in three spaces: a dining room (with an exit/entrance to the kitchen), a living room, and a balcony. The different spaces are arranged from stage right to left on a rotating platform. The action takes place in the centre of the stage.

Times and images are projected on the set.

NOTES

Names of people mentioned in dialogue can be updated/adapted.

All dialogue on the same horizontal line is to be spoken simultaneously.

A forward slash (/) indicates the beginning of the next line of dialogue.

Sentences without periods indicate that a line is unfinished or suspended.

You're either with us or against us
in the fight against terror.
—George W. Bush

So foul a sky clears not without a storm.
—King John, W. Shakespeare

ACT 1

1

OLIVIA watches the entrance to the kitchen as if she's worried a monster is about to leap out.

2

8:01 p.m. Dining room. ELIZABETH, JAMES, DANIEL, and MELISSA are all seated around a table. There's a bowl of fruit at the centre of the table. Plates, food, and wine glasses cover the rest of the table. They've finished eating. The sound of a TV drifts in from the living room. JAMES and MELISSA glance at each other. OLIVIA runs over to MELISSA, snuggling up to her.

ELIZABETH:	JAMES:	DANIEL:	MELISSA:
	Okay.		
(to OLIVIA) Oh hello, sweetie! Are you still hungry? Do you want Grandma to give you some chocolate? Some yummy chocolate?	So, Daniel		

ELIZABETH:	**JAMES:**	**DANIEL:**	**MELISSA:**
			(to ELIZABETH)
			No. Don't give
		(to JAMES)	her any choco-
		What?	late, Mom.
How about			
some cake?			
I made a nice			Mom, she just
cake for you!			had some.
How about			
some ice cream?			She's had three
Or strawberry			bowls. She's not
yogurt!			hungry any-
(to MELISSA)		What?	more, Mom.
Oh, please! It's	Pass me the wine.		
just strawberry			
yogurt!			
			It's still full of
			sugar!
No little girl has		*(DANIEL gives*	
ever died eating		*JAMES the bottle.)*	
strawberry	*(JAMES pours him-*		
yogurt	*self some wine.)*		
			Yeah, and I'm
			not that keen
			on her being the
(to JAMES)			first either!
I'm telling you,			
you can't even			
give kids a little			
treat these days.	*(to ELIZABETH)*		
	Oh, well I'm		
	sure you'll find		
	a way.		
Oh you better		*(DANIEL wants*	*(MELISSA looks off*
believe it!		*the bottle back.)*	*to the living room.)*

ELIZABETH:	**JAMES:**	**DANIEL:**	**MELISSA:**
	(to living room)		
(to OLIVIA*)* The next time you come over to Grandma's you can eat whatever you want! Until then, would you like a piece of fruit? Like an apple? A pear? A banana? A nice banana? Here, have a banana.	Hey! No! No! *(*JAMES *sets the bottle in front of himself.)*		
			Mom, it's not funny, okay! The last time you took care of her, she ate
		(to MELISSA*)* What do you expect? Mom was born right after the Great Depression. Fear of scarcity is in her genes.	an entire bag of candy. She had a stomach ache for three days! I was freaking out. Mom, stop! She's not hungry!
One banana!	*(to* OLIVIA*)* When your uncle Daniel was a little boy, Grandma wouldn't stop feeding him. He got so fat that he couldn't even fit through the doors anymore.		Okay, ONE banana.
Which banana do you want?			
		(to MELISSA*)* They're all the same size, Melissa.	The smallest one.
What is this? The army? Honestly. She can at least choose which banana she wants!			*(She looks at* DANIEL.*)*
		(to JAMES*)* What are you talking about?	*(to* ELIZABETH*)* You're the one who wants her to eat a banana, not her!
Oh, that's right. I'm manipulating her.			

ELIZABETH:	**JAMES:**	**DANIEL:**	**MELISSA:**
		Come on, this is stupid. She's right here. Let's ask her.	

DANIEL: Olivia, would you like to have a banana?

OLIVIA looks at ELIZABETH, then at MELISSA.

OLIVIA: Yes.

DANIEL: Which one would you like?

OLIVIA points at a banana.

OLIVIA: Gimme that one.

DANIEL pulls off a banana and gives it to OLIVIA.

MELISSA: What do you say?

OLIVIA: Thank you.

MELISSA: Thank you, *Daniel.*

DANIEL: Oh, you are so welcome.

MELISSA: Why don't you go play with Tyler in the living room? We're going to talk about grown-up stuff now, it'll be boring.

OLIVIA exits.

ELIZABETH:	**JAMES:**	**DANIEL:**	**MELISSA:**
Well, that was rude!			
	What? She said thank you.		
No. "Gimme."			No.
	What about it?		
She said gimme instead of give me.			I know.
	What's wrong with gimme?		
It's rude! It's very rude!		Come on, James.	
		You're supposed to say: "may I have" or "please give me."	
Goddammit! It makes me so angry! I hear it all the time, children at the store saying, "Gimme this, gimme that!"	Oh, right. Sure. Sorry.	She shouldn't say gimme or wanna or gonna or kinda. Unless maybe if she's with her friends.	I know, Mom. I've told her a thousand times.
Pointing. It makes me so mad! *(to DANIEL)* The other day,	Thanks, Daniel.		
Shaima	*(to MELISSA)* Who's that?	*(to ELIZABETH)* Yeah.	
Shaima wrote: "I went their—e-i-r." I told her,	*(JAMES pours wine for everyone except DANIEL.)*		*(to JAMES)* Shaima. The girl Mom helps with her homework.

ELIZABETH:	**JAMES:**	**DANIEL:**	**MELISSA:**
"Not e-i-r, e-r-e." And she says, "What do you mean?" "Because their, e-i-r, is a possessive pronoun and there, e-r-e, in this case, means a place you			
go to. Shaima went there—e-r-e." She says, "Why?" "Because that's	*(to MELISSA)* Shaima?		*(to JAMES)* It's Afghan.
how you write it, dear!" "Who decides that?" Right? If it were up to her there wouldn't be any grammar rules.			*(to ELIZABETH)* At least she didn't write "they're." They r-e. I see that all the time. Or "youse."
(to JAMES) Oh right, it's cool. It's so cool.	*(to ELIZABETH)* It's cool, mom.		
Everything has to be cool these days! *(to DANIEL)* Yesterday she comes to me and she says, "Liz, can	No, I mean about you helping her with her homework.		
I have a party at your house?" She calls me Liz, if	*(to MELISSA)* How long's she been doing this?		

ELIZABETH:	**JAMES:**	**DANIEL:**	**MELISSA:**
you can believe			*(to JAMES)*
that. I tell her,			Since fall.
“Why would	You must see		
you want to have	her a lot, Daniel.	*(to JAMES)*	
a party at my		Once in a while	
house?” And she	Do you help		
says, “So I can	her, too?		
have fun.” Can		Oh, I’m no	
you believe that?!		teacher.	*(to DANIEL)*
She wanted to			You’d be good at
invite her friends			teaching, actually
over here to have	Yes. Excellent.		
fun. No kidding,			
there’s twelve of			
them. They must			
really crack the			
whip over there.			
Her father never			
smiles—he won’t			
even look at me.			
He probably			
doesn’t under-			
stand a word of			
English.			
			Yeah, if they’re
			going to come
			here, they
			should at least
			start off by
			learning the
		(to MELISSA)	language.
		That’s exactly	
		what Shaima’s	*(to DANIEL)*
		doing.	Yeah, but not
			her father.

ELIZABETH:	**JAMES:**	**DANIEL:**	**MELISSA:**
		He's got twelve kids to feed!	
(to MELISSA*)* Melissa, sweetie, there's no way he's going to learn English here. Not in Toronto at least!			There's night classes for adults.
	(to ELIZABETH*)* Where's he going to learn it? Quebec?		
I don't know, but it's sure not going to happen if he's listening to the CBC. The girl who's on before the six o'clock news—you know, the one who . . .			
	(to ELIZABETH*)* Which one?		
Oh—I can't remember her name! It's terrible—she says—			
		Gill Deacon	
Gill! That's it! She says, "He was as calm as a cucumber."			

ELIZABETH:	**JAMES:**	**DANIEL:**	**MELISSA:**
	What's wrong		
(to JAMES)	with that?		
It's wrong! It's			
supposed to			
be "cool as a			
cucumber."		"Cool."	*(to ELIZABETH)*
	I know, Mom.		He's just trying
	I'm joking. I was		to rile you
(to MELISSA)	joking.	Calm!	up, Mom.
Well it worked!		*(to MELISSA)*	
Now I'm god-		Bob Cole used	
damn angry.		to say that a	
When I was		player "took a	
little	Well the arts	soft dump in the	
	reporter isn't the	corner."	*(to DANIEL)*
(to JAMES)	only one who	*(to MELISSA)*	He didn't.
When I was little	speaks like that.	I kid you not.	
	It's everybody in		
When	the media.	*(to JAMES)*	
When I was		No, that's not	
little, we listened		true. Matt	
to *John and Judy*		Galloway is very	
on the radio, and		articulate.	
it was very well	I don't listen		
written, I'll have	to him.		
you know.	*(to ELIZABETH)*	Gill Deacon, too.	
	That's totally	*(to MELISSA)*	Oh, she drives
	different, Mom!	And Steve Paikin	me nuts.
	You can't com-	is really articulate.	
	pare some arts		Yeah, but what
	program that's on		about the
	the CBC now with		accusations?
	a radio drama	He was cleared	
	from the forties!	of all that.	

ELIZABETH:	**JAMES:**	**DANIEL:**	**MELISSA:**
And why not?			Maybe, you
	The context is		never know.
	totally different!		
Exactly. What			Wasn't *John*
I'm saying is			*and Judy* a soap
people spoke			opera?
better before		You're prob-	
than they do		ably thinking	
today—and		of *Strange*	
people had very		*Paradise.*	
little education		That was the	
back then. So tell		Canadian ver-	
me how some		sion of *Dark*	
farmer who		*Shadows.*	
barely made it			Oh.
past grade five		There were tons	
spoke better		of reruns.	
than someone			Right.
graduating from		They shot a	
university today?		bit of it at	
Huh? How is		Casa Loma.	
that possible?			Cool.

JAMES gets up.

JAMES: *(at the entrance to the living room)* Ty! What did we say when we left the house? No phone at Grandma's! Don't make me sorry I bought you that thing or next it'll be no phone at home, no phone at your mom's, no phone anywhere! *(DANIEL pours himself some wine and places the bottle in front of himself.)* Don't you look at me like that. Put it away right now! I said now! *(Pause.)* And sit like a normal person and make some room for your cousin. Look, look, there's a big old TV right there in front of you. Why don't you watch that?

TYLER: *(from living room)* 'Cause there's nothing on!

JAMES: Then why don't you try something new and pull a book off the shelf? You know, a book? A bunch of pages inside two pieces of cardboard. No pictures, only words? There's two hundred and fifty of 'em right there behind you, so have at it. You'll see, *World of Warcraft* didn't come out of nowhere!

JAMES sits down again.

ELIZABETH:	**JAMES:**	**DANIEL:**	**MELISSA:**
	So,		
James, if you want, you can have the bookcase.	Daniel		
	Oh, thanks but I don't think I have the space for it.		Mom! You told me you were giving me the bookcase!
(to MELISSA) Then come over and get it!			
(to JAMES) It's too cramped in here for a bookcase like that.			Why are you in such a hurry to get rid of it? Far as I know, you're not moving anytime soon
	(to MELISSA) I can help you move it if you want		
		(to ELIZABETH) Your farmer may have been articulate, but he didn't know how to read or write.	
Oh, because all the students			

ELIZABETH:	**JAMES:**	**DANIEL:**	**MELISSA:**
coming out of university nowadays know how to write, do they?			
		Generally speaking, people are more edu- cated today than they were fifty years ago.	
	I don't think so.		
Says who?			
(to DANIEL)		There are studies.	
What's the point	Studies?		
of being more educated if no one is capable of			
writing a single	Where did you		
sentence without	read that?	*(to JAMES)*	
there being ten		In the paper.	
mistakes in it?	Which paper?		
(to JAMES)		The *National Post*.	
Look at Shaima	Well, that's a reliable source.		
		It was an inde-	
(to MELISSA)		pendent study	
Look at Shaima	I'll do an inde- pendent study for you.		

JAMES: Ty?

TYLER: *(from living room)* What.

JAMES: Come here.

TYLER: *(from living room)* What!

JAMES: Come here.

TYLER enters the dining room.

What's the capital of Ontario? Toronto or Ottawa?

TYLER: Why?

JAMES: Just 'cause— What's the capital of Ontario? Toronto or Ottawa?

ELIZABETH: Come on, James. He knows what the capital of Ontario is, really.

JAMES: Shush. What's the capital of Ontario?

TYLER: Of Ontario?

JAMES: Yes.

TYLER: It's—uh. I don't know.

JAMES: Thank you.

TYLER goes back to the living room.

See? He doesn't even know what the capital of Ontario is.

ELIZABETH:	**JAMES:**	**DANIEL:**	**MELISSA:**
	(to DANIEL*)*		
	And you're		
	telling me that		
	people are more		
	educated now		
(to MELISSA*)*	than before		
Look at Shaima:			
they don't	The *National Post*		
even give kids			
spelling tests			
anymore! And			
when they do,			
they get to use	Every time I		
a dictionary. I	read Jonathan		*(to* ELIZABETH*)*
mean, come on,	Kay it really		That's not
what's next?	makes me want		true, Mom.
What isn't true?	to bomb the		
	National Post.	*(to* JAMES*)*	No elementary
		There are some	school teacher
		journalists at	lets the kids use a
		the *Post* who are	dictionary during
		actually much	spelling tests.
Shaima told me!		more indepen-	
		dent-minded	Maybe that's
	Independent-	than at the *Globe.*	because
	minded? Just		Shaima's behind.
No, it's not only	because you		*(*MELISSA *looks off*
her, it's all the	put a bunch		*toward the living*
students!	of contrarians		*room.)*
	together and let		I don't think
(to JAMES*)*	them say what-	When you read	so, Mom.
God, she's so	ever they want	someone like	
pigheaded!	doesn't mean	Tanya Talaga, you	Anyway, that's
	they're indepen-	can't say that's too	not what I do.
	dent-minded.	objective either.	

ELIZABETH:	JAMES:	DANIEL:	MELISSA:
Well good for you, dear!	No. But at least it's not all op-eds and hot takes! *(to living room)* Ty! What the hell are you doing? You're going to break her arm!		*(OLIVIA shrieks. MELISSA frowns.)* They're only allowed to use dictionaries when they correct their work.
(to DANIEL) See! What did I tell you? They get to correct their own work!		Maybe read it for yourself. Then you'll see it's not all op-eds and hot takes.	
	(to DANIEL) When all a newspaper talks about is *The Voice*, hospital wait times, and dogs that got run over when there's thousands of people protesting in the streets, then that's a fucking problem.		It's the only way they'll learn what mistakes they're making, Mom. Or else they won't see them. What do you want us to do? It doesn't sink into their heads.
Yes, that's it. What can you do, dear? What can you do? No one's responsible for anything these days, especially not for young people! I mean seriously			
	(to MELISSA) They can't even hear us.	I'm not saying it's the best newspaper in the world. I'm just trying to get my news from different sources, that's all.	*(to JAMES)* Please, James, stop swearing.
			Doesn't matter.
All this education reform, "don't mean	*(JAMES pours himself some wine.)*		

ELIZABETH:	JAMES:	DANIEL:	MELISSA:
shit" as the kids say, does it?			
			And whose fault is that?
	Kathleen Wynne's.		
		Oh, everything started way before her.	
Listen, dearies, it's not that complicated. You were never taught grammar. Daniel's the only one of you kids who can write without making mistakes.			
			True. Dan writes very well.
And I have no idea why. It's not like he ever studied.			
	Well, he had to study a little to pass the bar exam.		
		I studied.	
Not much. Not in elementary school.			
		That, I'll admit.	
	He couldn't— he needed time		

ELIZABETH:	**JAMES:**	**DANIEL:**	**MELISSA:**
	to practise his Pierre Trudeau imitation.		*(She laughs.)*
Good old Petro Pete!			Oh, that's right!
	With his cute little suit: "If		
He was good at it, too.	Canada is to survive, it can only survive in mutual respect and in love for one another."		
		"In mutual respect and in love for one another."	
(She laughs.)	He even tried to grow sideburns		*(She laughs.)* Right! And he had that wide
	He was what? Eight or nine at most?		tie! Damn, that was so funny!
It was funny. Much funnier than the original, that's for sure.			
		(to ELIZABETH*)* What do you mean?	
(to DANIEL*)* Trudeau was a tyrant. He basically radicalized an entire population. During the October			*(to* JAMES*)* I remember, whenever Dad went away for the weekend to go to some workshop or

ELIZABETH:	JAMES:	DANIEL:	MELISSA:
Crisis, he arrested			conference, he
everybody and			always took Dan
anybody except			along with him.
the actual terror-	He called him		
ists. "Just watch	"my little prince."		
me!" We watched			Dan always
him all right.			packed his
He pandered to			pyjamas in a
Quebec, tried to			black suitcase—
buy their votes.			remember that
And it certainly			vinyl suitcase,
cost him—and			with the combi-
us. And created			nation lock?
a huge divide in	Yeah, yeah, yeah.		
this country when			And for the
there wasn't one.			entire week-
		He didn't back	end he strolled
		down. No other	through the halls
		prime minis-	of the hotel in his
		ter would have	suit and tie, carry-
		done that. At	ing that suitcase.
		least he had a	Up and down the
		backbone.	elevator. Playing
Oh, please! That			diplomat.
was all for show.	Living high on		
A way for him	the hog.		
to demonstrate			Everyone was so
to the rest of			impressed with
the country			how articulate
that we were all			he was. He had
united against a			political opin-
common enemy.			ions. He spoke
A gang of des-		They were	really well for his
perate teenagers?		terrorists.	age. I remember
Oh, please! Who		In their twenties.	how people in

ELIZABETH:	**JAMES:**	**DANIEL:**	**MELISSA:**
imposes martial law when a tiny group of idealistic kids—petty criminals!—do			my class would say, "One day your brother's going to be prime minister!"
something completely idiotic?	They were just teasing you.		
And then they used the opportunity to		They took hostages!	Sure, but they were jealous of him too.
round up all the	Maybe.		
"bleeding hearts" that didn't agree with them. Tell me, what was the		There were bombs. They murdered someone.	Dan was really smart for his age. Anyway, smarter than average,
point of all that?	*(to* DANIEL*)*		that's for sure.
	Goes to show you that you need more than that to be successful.	To defend the country	
		Multiculturalism	
			And if you
		Federal unity	think about the
Oh, please don't give me that federal unity crap.			kind of people that were around us back
		Which arose out of a vision for society, mostly	then—I mean, the Pattersons! Remember them? What
Unions, you mean.		left-leaning, that included all the people in this country. Don't you think	idiots. No one in that house ever cracked a book. The father drank

ELIZABETH:	**JAMES:**	**DANIEL:**	**MELISSA:**
		that was worth fighting for?	and beat his kids!
	I don't remember that.		
I don't know. I think he was just looking out for his legacy. And for what? Who do you think was responsible for Harper?			We were lucky to have the childhood we had, that's for sure!
	(to ELIZABETH*)* Didn't you vote for Trudeau?		
(to JAMES*)* That's none of your business.			
		Come on, Mom, it's been over forty years. You can tell us.	
No, I'm not telling you.			
	You voted Conservative?		
Sure, I voted for good old Lyin' Brian.			
			(to JAMES*)* She's always voted NDP, you know that.
There was this one guy at the hospital, a real card-carrying union man, the local rep—and, well if he was			

ELIZABETH:	JAMES:	DANIEL:	MELISSA:
supposed to finish his shift at five—right, Michael!—well at 4:45, he was already out of his uniform. And he still managed to whine about his pay and working conditions! Well, let me tell you, that made me sick to my stomach.		Wasn't his name Michael?	
			(to DANIEL*)* How do you remember that?
		(to MELISSA*)* I must've gone to visit Mom at the hospital—I don't know—I just remember it.	
			You've really got a memory like an elephant
	Wasn't he a homosexual?		
			(to DANIEL*)* What difference does it make, James?
Come to think of it, he was. And he spent a lot of time trying to convince us that we were too. Because you know, for the gays, everybody's gay, right? And don't bother telling them otherwise. If you make the mistake of saying you're straight, they'll try to prove to you that you're a repressed homo.			
	(to MELISSA*)* What? I just remember that he was a homosexual. He had a lisp.		
			So?
	So nothing. I just remembered, that's all.		
			*(*MELISSA *looks off toward the living room.* OLIVIA *comes into the dining room.)*

MELISSA: What's the matter, sweetheart?

OLIVIA: Tyler won't let me watch TV.

JAMES: Tyler!

TYLER: *(from living room)* What? I didn't do anything!

JAMES: Hey, smartass! You're not back home in the basement! Let her watch whatever she wants.

TYLER: *(from living room)* But she wasn't even watching!

OLIVIA: I was too.

TYLER: *(from living room)* Well, if you were watching, then we don't have to change the channel!

MELISSA: / Do you want us to go play in the park?

JAMES: Okay, that's enough. Turn off the TV, Ty!

OLIVIA shakes her head.

MELISSA: You sure?

OLIVIA nods.

JAMES: Ty, don't make me come in there!

TYLER: *(from living room)* Fuck!

JAMES gets up, goes into the living room, and turns off the TV.

JAMES: Excuse me? You change your attitude right now and calm down or we're going home, you got that?!

ELIZABETH: After Grandma does the dishes / we'll all watch TV together, okay, sweet pea?

JAMES: *(from living room)* What was that?

JAMES enters with TYLER's phone in hand.

You know what this is? The end of civilization as we know it.

3

The platform rotates, turning from the dining room to the living room.

8:01 p.m. Living room. A huge hardwood bookcase lines the back wall. It is overflowing with books. TYLER *watches* TV, *seated on the couch. We faintly, but distinctly, hear the adults' voices coming in from the dining room (the same conversation as in Scene 2).*

TYLER *glances toward the dining room, then pulls out a cellphone that was hidden beneath him. He pretends to watch* TV *while playing a game on his phone.*

JAMES: *(from dining room, to* TYLER*)* Hey! No! No!

TYLER *puts his phone away reluctantly. He flips through the channels, annoyed. He tosses the remote aside, giving up.*

OLIVIA *enters the living room with a banana. At the end of* ELIZABETH*'s line: "The other day, Shaima wrote: I went their —e-i-r,"* OLIVIA *goes to sit down.*

TYLER: I wouldn't sit there if I was you.

OLIVIA: Why?

TYLER: There's a rat inside the couch.

OLIVIA: Huh?

TYLER: There's a rat that lives inside the couch.

OLIVIA: No way.

TYLER: There's a rat that lives here at Grandma's. You didn't know that?

OLIVIA: Then why are you sitting on the couch?

TYLER: Because I'm not sitting on the side where the rat is.

OLIVIA: I don't believe you.

TYLER: Whatever. Suit yourself.

OLIVIA hesitates, then sits on the arm of the couch. She peels her banana.

After ELIZABETH's line: "Melissa, sweetie, there's no way he's going to learn English here. Not in Toronto at least!" TYLER continues.

You're going to attract the rat with your banana.

OLIVIA: Rats don't eat bananas.

TYLER: Rats eat everything. If a rat's trapped, it'll do anything to get away. It'll eat a path right through whatever's in front of it.

OLIVIA: As if.

TYLER: Don't believe me? They already did this experiment, okay? They put a guy's face inside a cage—with a rat in it. Then, they lit one side of the cage on fire. The rat didn't have a choice. It had to dig an exit or get burnt alive, so it ate the guy's face off.

OLIVIA: Eww, gross!

OLIVIA eats her banana, losing her appetite with each bite. TYLER pretends to watch TV while playing a game on his phone. OLIVIA doesn't finish the banana. She goes and hides the uneaten portion in the bookcase, then comes back to sit on the arm of the couch as JAMES bursts in.

JAMES: Ty! What did we say when we left the house? No phone at Grandma's! Don't make me sorry I bought you that thing or next it'll be no phone at home, no phone at your mom's, no phone anywhere!

TYLER looks at JAMES with total contempt.

Don't you look at me like that. Put it away right now! I said now!

TYLER grudgingly puts his phone away.

And sit like a normal person and make some room for your cousin.

TYLER sits up coolly. OLIVIA sits tentatively.

Look, look, there's a big old TV right there in front of you. Why don't you watch that?

TYLER: *(tossing the remote)* 'Cause there's nothing on!

OLIVIA picks up the remote.

JAMES: Then why don't you try something new and pull a book off the shelf? You know, a book? A bunch of pages inside two pieces of cardboard. No pictures, only words? There's two hundred and fifty of 'em right there behind you, so have at it. You'll see, *World of Warcraft* didn't come out of nowhere!

JAMES goes back to the dining room.

TYLER: *(to himself)* I haven't even played that game in like ten years.

After DANIEL'*s line "People are more educated . . . "* TYLER *takes the remote from* OLIVIA.

OLIVIA: Hey!

TYLER: You had your turn.

TYLER *changes the channel.*

OLIVIA: I was watching that.

TYLER: It was boring.

TYLER *flips the channels mechanically.*

OLIVIA: Tyler, you're not even watching. Give it back!

JAMES: *(from dining room)* Ty?

TYLER: What.

JAMES: *(from dining room)* Come here.

TYLER: What!

JAMES: *(from dining room)* Come here.

TYLER *goes to the dining room.* OLIVIA *sits in* TYLER'*s spot, picks up the remote, and changes the channel.*

What's the capital of Ontario? Toronto or Ottawa?

TYLER: *(from dining room)* Why?

JAMES: *(from dining room)* Just 'cause— What's the capital of Ontario? Toronto or Ottawa?

ELIZABETH: *(from dining room)* Come on, James. He knows what the capital of Ontario is, really.

JAMES: *(from dining room)* Shush. What's the capital of Ontario?

TYLER: *(from dining room)* Of Ontario?

JAMES: *(from dining room)* Yes.

TYLER: *(from dining room)* It's—uh. I don't know.

JAMES: *(from dining room)* Thank you.

TYLER comes back to the living room.

TYLER: Move.

OLIVIA: Why?

TYLER: Move!

OLIVIA: Are you scared of the rat?

TYLER: I said move.

OLIVIA doesn't budge. TYLER sits on her. Pause. They watch TV.

OLIVIA: Tyler, get off me.

TYLER: Man, am I ever comfortable.

OLIVIA: Tyler, get up, I can't breathe.

TYLER: That's weird, I think the couch is talking to me.

OLIVIA: Tyler!

TYLER: Louder, I can't hear you.

TYLER puts more of his weight into the couch. He leaps up and looks at the bite mark on his arm.

Do you have rabies or something?

OLIVIA: You taste gross, you disgusting pig!

TYLER: Disgusting pig?

OLIVIA: You disgusting pig!

TYLER grabs OLIVIA by the arm. She lets out a piercing scream.

JAMES: *(from dining room)* Ty! What the hell are you doing? You're going to break her arm!

TYLER lets her go.

TYLER: You little shit.

TYLER pretends he's going to pounce on OLIVIA. She runs away. TYLER sprawls out on the couch and starts flipping through channels again. OLIVIA sits on the arm of the couch. Pause. They watch TV. After ELIZABETH's line "Especially not for young people . . . " TYLER continues.

Fuck, the TV sucks at Grandma's!

OLIVIA: I'm going to tell that you swore.

TYLER: Why doesn't she have Netflix?

OLIVIA: She has cable, but it's not really cable.

At the end of ELIZABETH*'s line "Daniel's the only one of you kids who can write without making mistakes"* TYLER *continues.*

TYLER: How can you even live like this?

OLIVIA: She watches TV to help her fall asleep.

TYLER: This fucking sucks! And the remote is so gross. There's brown stuff between the buttons. I bet she took a dump on it.

OLIVIA: I'm going to tell.

TYLER: What, it's possible. I saw it on the news. Some old guy went to the bathroom but never came back. They found him on the floor lying in his own shit. Like he keeled over right before making it to the toilet.

OLIVIA: *(indicating the remote)* Give it.

On ELIZABETH*'s line "Funnier than the original . . . "* TYLER *continues.*

TYLER: Have you seen *Off Their Rockers*?

OLIVIA: No.

TYLER: Okay, so this old lady's in a dog park. She goes up to this girl who's on a bench and asks her for some paper. The girl says, "What for?" The old lady says, "I need to take a shit."

OLIVIA *laughs.*

In another one, this old guy is in a high school and asks this girl to help him find his class. The girl says, "What class is it?" And the old guy says, "Cunnilingus 101."

OLIVIA *doesn't react.*

In this other one, this old lady's walking through a park. When she sees these two guys she says, "Would you please stop staring at my tits?"

OLIVIA: Okay, give it.

After ELIZABETH*'s line "Do something completely idiotic . . . "* TYLER *continues.*

TYLER: Did you see the last *Jackass* movie?

OLIVIA: No.

TYLER: Okay, so this guy puts on this super realistic old man disguise and then he does all sorts of stupid stuff, like shoplifting, smashing into stuff with a car, grabbing girls' butts. He does everything with this short fat kid, who's like his grandson, and everyone freaks.

OLIVIA: Oh yeah, I saw it.

TYLER: No you didn't.

OLIVIA: Yeah I did.

TYLER: Oh yeah, what's it called?

OLIVIA: I don't know but I saw it.

TYLER: Shut up, you didn't see it.

After JAMES*'s line "Didn't you vote for . . . ?"* TYLER *continues.*

So the old guy signs his grandson up for this beauty contest for little girls. Then the grandson—who's dressed like a girl—starts doing this super cheesy routine, dancing to this music for babies, then the music changes and the grandson rips his dress off and starts doing a pole dance to some heavy metal with smoke and everything. Then the grandfather gets up on stage and stuffs a couple of twenties into his G-string.

OLIVIA: Give it, it's my turn.

TYLER: No.

OLIVIA: You're not even watching.

TYLER: I know.

OLIVIA: Then give it!

TYLER: No.

OLIVIA tries to take the remote. TYLER pushes her away. At the end of ELIZABETH's line "That made me sick . . . " OLIVIA keeps going.

OLIVIA: Tyler, give me the remote.

TYLER: Shh, I'm trying to watch TV.

TYLER looks at the TV. OLIVIA looks at him, seething. At the end of ELIZABETH's line "If you make the mistake of saying you're straight . . . " she goes into the dining room.

MELISSA: *(from dining room)* What's the matter, sweetheart?

OLIVIA: *(from dining room)* Tyler won't let me watch TV.

JAMES: *(from dining room)* Tyler!

TYLER: What? I didn't do anything!

JAMES: *(from dining room)* Hey, smartass! You're not back home in the basement! Let her watch whatever she wants.

TYLER: But she wasn't even watching!

OLIVIA: *(from dining room)* I was too!

TYLER: Well, if you were watching, then we don't have to change the channel!

MELISSA: *(from dining room)* Do you want us to go play in the park?

JAMES: *(from dining room)* Okay, that's enough. Turn off the TV, Ty!

MELISSA: *(from dining room)* You sure?

JAMES: *(from dining room)* Ty, don't make me come in there!

TYLER: Fuck!

JAMES comes into the living room.

JAMES: Excuse me?

TYLER turns off the TV.

You change your attitude right now and calm down or we're going home, you got that?!

TYLER: I don't care.

JAMES: What was that?

TYLER: Nothing.

JAMES: Right.

JAMES takes TYLER's phone and exits.

(from dining room) You know what this is? The end of civilization as we know it.

OLIVIA comes back to the living room. TYLER looks at her, seething.

TYLER: I'm gonna kill you. I'm gonna cut you up into little pieces and I'm going to feed you to the rat.

OLIVIA: Yum yum, lucky rat.

4

The platform rotates from the living room to the balcony. Two empty flowerpots are attached to the railing. There is a planter with dead plants, a broom, and a tree branch. OLIVIA *opens the sliding door. Wind blows the branch, and its shadow moves over the balcony.* OLIVIA *looks at the branch, as if a monster were about to leap out.*

8:13 p.m. Pause. Something moves on the branch. OLIVIA *freezes.* SQUIRREL *appears on the branch. Pause. It runs and stops at the tip of the branch. Pause.* SQUIRREL *jumps from the branch onto the railing.* OLIVIA *backs away. Pause.* SQUIRREL *rummages in the flowerpot. He finds a cigarette butt and turns it over in his paws before dropping it. Pause.* SQUIRREL *gets on its hind legs and sniffs in* OLIVIA*'s direction.*

OLIVIA *approaches slowly.* SQUIRREL *backs away. She holds out her hand.*

OLIVIA: Tsk-tsk-tsk. Don't be scared. I won't hurt you.

SQUIRREL *gets closer and sniffs* OLIVIA*'s hand from afar.*

Hold on. Don't move.

OLIVIA *goes inside the apartment.* SQUIRREL *looks off toward the living room.* OLIVIA *comes back onto the balcony, throws the banana peel into a flowerpot, and holds out a piece of the banana for* SQUIRREL.

Tsk-tsk-tsk. Here, eat this.

SQUIRREL approaches, takes the piece of banana, and turns it over in its paws. It gets up on its hind legs and eats.

Good, huh?

SQUIRREL drops the piece of banana and freezes.

What? You don't want any more? You full?

TYLER comes onto the balcony. SQUIRREL backs away.

TYLER: What are you doing?

OLIVIA: Nothing.

TYLER: You were feeding the squirrel, I saw you.

OLIVIA: No.

TYLER: Squirrels don't eat bananas.

OLIVIA: He ate some.

TYLER: If you wanna catch it, you gotta give it nuts.

OLIVIA: I don't want to catch it.

TYLER approaches. SQUIRREL backs away to the opposite end of the balcony.

What are you doing?

TYLER: I thought you didn't want to catch it.

OLIVIA: I don't want to scare it either!

TYLER: Check this out.

TYLER moves aggressively toward the rodent. SQUIRREL runs away.

OLIVIA: Stop it!

TYLER: He's so fucking stupid.

SQUIRREL tries to reach the branch by crawling along the wall. TYLER picks up the broom.

Oh he's not going anywhere.

OLIVIA: Stop! You'll make him fall!

TYLER tries to hit the rodent. SQUIRREL lets out an irate screech at TYLER.

TYLER: Oh yeah, huh?

TYLER tries to hit it again. SQUIRREL grabs hold of the broom.

You're fucking dead, man.

TYLER whacks the broom against the railing. SQUIRREL falls into the darkness. TYLER watches him fall, satisfied. OLIVIA's horrified.

OLIVIA: Why'd you do that? He didn't do anything to you!

TYLER: He fucking tried to bite me.

OLIVIA rains punches on TYLER.

Are you fucking crazy!

OLIVIA: I'm going to tell your dad!

TYLER: You say one word and I'll kill you.

ACT 2

1

The platform rotates from the balcony to the dining room. OLIVIA *looks at* TYLER *with loathing.*

2

8:24 p.m. Dining room. DANIEL, JAMES, *and* MELISSA *are seated around the table. A second bottle of wine has been opened.* MELISSA *is watching a video on* TYLER*'s phone.* JAMES *looks at her, awaiting her reaction.* ELIZABETH *clears the table.*

ELIZABETH:	JAMES:	DANIEL:	MELISSA:
(to DANIEL*)* And I suppose you're going to tell me he wasn't responsible?			
		(to ELIZABETH*)* He's responsible, but not for that.	
If I owned a trucking company and one of my trucks killed an entire hockey team, I wouldn't be so smug.			

ELIZABETH:	JAMES:	DANIEL:	MELISSA:
		He wasn't smug.	
Well he sure looked it.			
		You can't judge someone based on how they do or don't look, Mom.	
Okay, so tell me, what do you base your judgment on?			
		On facts.	
Oh, really? And what do the facts say? That the company was cutting corners!			
And where did they make cuts? Safety and training, obviously! What are security regulations for anyway? To protect dummies like us from all the disasters out there!		You don't know that.	
Because some guy who owns a fleet of trucks doesn't give a crap, that's for damn sure!		That's your interpretation of the facts.	

ELIZABETH:	**JAMES:**	**DANIEL:**	**MELISSA:**
		I agree with you,	It doesn't prove
		but the owner	anything.
	What do you	wasn't the one	
	mean it doesn't	who crashed	
	prove anything?	the truck into	
	Can't you see it?	the bus.	
What are you	Building seven		
trying to say?	collapses while		
	all the other	That there were	
	buildings next	a lot of different	
	to it aren't even	factors at play.	
But he owned	touched.		
the truck. He let			It got hit with
the driver skip		The intersection	debris from the
the safety checks.		was dangerous	Twin Towers.
He should be the	It's impossible		
one going to jail.	for a forty-		
	seven-storey	It's much more	
	building to fall	complicated	
	straight down	than that, Mom.	
That's right, it's	like that just		
complicated!	because it gets		
And mean-	hit with some		
while, no one's	debris. Look.		
responsible for	*(He replays the*		
anything! Even	*video.)*		
when it's plain			
as the nose on			
your face!			
			But you can see
			it, there, there's
			a fire!
	Even if you set		
	a skyscraper		
	on fire, it still		

ELIZABETH:	JAMES:	DANIEL:	MELISSA:
	won't fall. For a tower like that to go straight down, you need to dynamite it from the bottom, okay.		Whatever, fine.
			Why would anyone do that?
	Do you know what was on the first floor of building seven?		
			No?
	The headquarters of the CIA.		
			Yeah so?
	What do you mean, "Yeah, so?" They wanted to get rid of compromising evidence.		
			What evidence?
	Evidence of the truth!		
It's like that guy. The maniac—			Isn't that kind of a stretch?
	It's not a stretch. I think it's pretty obvious, actually.	The maniac?	
The one who escaped.			
		Which one?	
The one with the meat cleaver. He's			Sorry, James, but I don't believe it.

ELIZABETH:	**JAMES:**	**DANIEL:**	**MELISSA:**
scary looking			
. . . Dong!	You need to		
	start asking	Oh you	
	questions,	mean Cong.	
He chops up his	Melissa. Inform		
roommate into	yourself.		Oh, I'm
pieces. He gets			informed, James,
caught right		He didn't chop	don't worry.
after. Covered in	Well, not if	him up, but sure.	
blood. Holding	you're reading		
the cleaver. He	newspapers and		
even says he did	watching TV,		
it! Then, after,	you aren't.		Oh no? Then
we're supposed			tell me, how do
to believe it's			I get informed,
not his fault?			James?
	By doing your	Nobody said	
	own research.	it wasn't his	
		fault. He wasn't	On the Internet?
	For instance.	criminally	
		responsible	I thought it
		because of a	was the end of
		mental disorder.	civilization?
A mental dis-	Not if you know		
order, right!	how to use it!		
How conve-	*(He pours himself*		
nient. Especially	*some wine.)*		
after people			
find out you've			
done some-			
thing wrong. I			
wouldn't be sur-			
prised if Doug	Who does the		
Ford tries using	Bank of Canada		
that as an excuse	belong to?		

ELIZABETH:	**JAMES:**	**DANIEL:**	**MELISSA:**
for losing all that money selling marijuana.			Is this a trick question?
	Just answer. Who does the Bank of Canada belong to?		
			Canadians.
	No. The Bank of Canada belongs to the Canadian banks, which are all private corporations.		
And there's the other guy.			
	(JAMES drinks.)	Which other guy?	
The child killer from Quebec. I've met more than my share of doctors and normally they're level-headed people.		You mean Turcotte.	Mm-hmm.
		So?	
So, after you kill your kids, it's easy to say that you were temporarily insane!	Do you know when the last financial crisis was?		So?
			Jeez, what is this, a pop quiz? 2008.

ELIZABETH:	JAMES:	DANIEL:	MELISSA:
	Do you know		
	how much		
	profit the big six		
	Canadian banks		
	made in 2009?		
			Millions.
	Fourteen point	Let's say he was	
	four billion!	fully aware of	
	The entire world	what he was	
	is falling apart	doing during the	
	and the banks	murders.	
Sure. I can	make 14.4 bil-		
say that, no	lion in profit!		
problem.	Do you know		
	how high our	Well, just	
	national debt is?	because you're	
	Eight hundred	aware of some-	
	billion. And that	thing doesn't	
	means 160 mil-	mean you're	
	lion in interest	in control of	
	a day, which is	your actions.	
	sixty billion a	It's like you're	
	year! And who	observing	
	gets that sweet	yourself doing	
	sixty billion?	what you're	
		doing. It's	The banks.
	Exactly. And you	neurological.	
"It's not my fault,	won't read any-		
Your Honour,	thing about that		
my brain did it"?	in the papers.		
		I read a study	
		about it. It hap-	
		pens in a specific	
		area of the brain.	
		Most people	

ELIZABETH:	JAMES:	DANIEL:	MELISSA:
		who commit murder have an underdeveloped prefrontal cortex.	
So they just have to cut out a bit of brain and poof, "You're free to go, sir, all your sins are forgiven"?			
		No, that's not what I'm saying.	
	Have you ever heard of the Bilderberg Group?		
			I think you might have mentioned it.
	It's this group of 120 people who meet every year, right? In the group are CEOs of international organizations like the IMF, leaders of the most industrial-ized countries,		
So even if what you're saying is true, do you	billionaires like Galen Weston and David		

ELIZABETH:	JAMES:	DANIEL:	MELISSA:
think that a brain operation could get rid of someone's desire to kill?	Rockefeller. We're talking about 120 people who control all the wealth and resources on the planet.	Of course it would. But it would be harmful.	
Harmful to who?			
Harmful to us, the idiots who are going to have to pay for the operation with our taxes, that's who.		Harmful to them!	
		All right! So, if it weren't for the money, you'd be in favour of lobotomizing people again?	
You brought up brains, not me.			
	You know why we never hear about it?		
			About what?
	About the Bilderberg Group.		
			Uh—because no one cares?

ELIZABETH:	**JAMES:**	**DANIEL:**	**MELISSA:**
	No. Because they control all the media: TV stations, newspapers like the *New York Times*, the *Washington Post*, the banks, the oil companies,		
Anyway, we wouldn't be talking about all this if they hadn't let that child killer off.	and the UN. We're talking about 120 people who are actually a super government		
	that decides which country will prosper, which will collapse, which president to	Turcotte's back in jail, Mom. He's serving a life sentence for second-degree murder.	
Well, they'll probably let him out early for good behaviour. And he's probably staying at a sweat lodge anyway.	elect. Obama's victory, JFK's assassination, all that was decided in advance.		
		He's in a federal penitentiary. He already tried to kill himself once. Every move he makes is being watched.	

ELIZABETH:	JAMES:	DANIEL:	MELISSA:
And right after he gets out, first thing you'll know is he's married again and his wife is having have a baby.		No way.	
		It won't happen.	
What won't happen?			
		I don't think he's going to get married again so fast.	
Why wouldn't he?			
	Have you ever heard of Malthusianism?		
			No.
It happens. There are women who fall in love with men straight out of prison simply because they had their picture in the paper.	It's a policy that advocates for population control. It's pretty obvious that the Bilderberg Group's goal is to shrink the world's population to five hundred million. We're talking about eliminating ninety percent of the	Like who?	

ELIZABETH:	**JAMES:**	**DANIEL:**	**MELISSA:**
I don't know.	people living on		
Some serial killer.	this planet!		
		Turcotte	
		isn't a serial	
	Do you know	killer, Mom.	
Oh no? Then	how they're		
what do you call	going to do it?		
someone who			No.
stabs one child	By creating		
to death, then	epidemics! But		
stabs their other	epidemics aren't		
child, killing	what's danger-		
them too? How	ous, no, it's the		
many until we're	vaccines! During		
in serial ter-	an epidemic,		
ritory? Three?	everybody		
Four? Ten? Isn't	panics and runs	That's not the	
it? Do we have	to get a vac-	point.	
to wait until he	cine that's got		
kills twenty kids	long-term side		
before we say a	effects, ones		
guy like that is	that make you		
dangerous?	infertile. When	Okay, so then	
	I was young, no	what are you	
	one got vacci-	proposing?	
People like that	nated for the flu.		
belong in prison.	Now everyone's		
	getting vacci-	He is in prison.	
Now. But first he	nated every few		
went to a mental	months!		
institution!	Since COVID,		
	SARS, the	Because, at the	
	swine flu . . . I	time, they said	
	mean—when	he wasn't crimi-	
	you really think	nally responsible.	

ELIZABETH:	JAMES:	DANIEL:	MELISSA:
But he admitted to killing his kids! How can they say he wasn't criminally responsible?	about it, it's already started!		*(to DANIEL)* I agree.
		(to ELIZABETH) Anyway, they changed their minds. Now he's in prison for life.	
Only for seventeen years! And when he gets out, we'll have to babysit him until the day he dies!			
		(to ELIZABETH) What did you want? For them to hang him in the town square?	
I don't know, but now every scumbag criminal is laughing in our faces, claiming they're not responsible.			
	(to DANIEL) Exactly.		
		Do you seriously think he wanted to kill	

ELIZABETH:	**JAMES:**	**DANIEL:**	**MELISSA:**
		his children? Didn't you feel like killing us sometimes?	
Oh please, Daniel! What does that have to do with anything?!			
		I'm only talking about a feeling.	
Stop it. You're going to make me angry!	Have you ever heard of the HAARP project?		
		It's a hypothetical question, Mom.	
			No, and you know what? I don't want to.
You know what I think about you and your questions!			
	Oh well, if you'd rather stay in the dark, that's up to you.		
			Really, and what do you do with all your knowledge, James?
	I communicate it, Melissa. I share it. I get it out there.		
		When James lit his bed on fire, didn't you feel like killing him?	

ELIZABETH:	**JAMES:**	**DANIEL:**	**MELISSA:**
Okay, that's it. I've had enough.			
	I didn't light my bed on fire.		
		(to JAMES) Yes, James, you lit your bed on fire.	
			Huh, when was this?
	(to MELISSA) I fell asleep smoking a cigarette.		
(to JAMES) Smoking joints!			
	One joint.		
			Huh, I didn't know about this!
	I wasn't actu-ally smoking it. I was just a little kid!		
		Yeah, right!	
			Jesus. How old were you?
Oh god.		Eight.	
			Eight years old? Wow!
	Melissa, get over it. Everyone smoked.		
Not everyone.			
	Dad smoked.		
			Dad smoked?
Look, kids, your father may not be a saint, but he never smoked a joint in his life.			

ELIZABETH:	JAMES:	DANIEL:	MELISSA:
	Oh come on, Mom! He sat around in a circle with Vishnu, Mary-Moon, Ganesh, and some other hippies, and they passed around these cones as big as baseball bats! Oh yeah and—Mamagaya! What was her real name?		
		Louise Rogers.	
	Yeah, Mamagaya a.k.a. Louise Rogers! What a piece of work! She was always trying to get Mom to let us walk around in the nude.		
In the middle of November! Seriously!			
			Where the hell was I?
James	Completely naked, being rocked to sleep by Gaya Rogers.		

ELIZABETH:	JAMES:	DANIEL:	MELISSA:
		Didn't she try to nurse Melissa once?	
I wouldn't have let her!			
*(*ELIZABETH *takes the glass out of* JAMES*'s hand.)* Okay, James. That's enough. I might not have been a perfect mother, but I did my best to protect all of you. The commune may have taken my husband from me, but one thing's for certain, there was no room for violence under my roof. So even when you're totally pissed off at your eight-year-old who just about set the house on fire, nothing can justify physically harming	I don't remember if she tried, but I sure remember her boobs. *(makes a gesture)* What?		

ELIZABETH:	JAMES:	DANIEL:	MELISSA:
him! You hear me? Nothing! If people killed			
their children every time they got upset, there wouldn't be anyone left.		We're talking about people with serious psychotic disorders, Mom.	
Right! Poor him. He lost it because he got dumped! Me too. I thought I was losing it a couple of times, but I didn't wake you up and stab you.			
		Lucky us!	
And by the way, you might not know this, but the first thing you learn when you're a parent is to control your anger.			
		Who said anything about anger?	
That's what he said in court!			
		So what? Maybe it wasn't just anger. Maybe	

ELIZABETH:	**JAMES:**	**DANIEL:**	**MELISSA:**
		it was—I don't	
		know—com-	
		passion.	
Really, Daniel,	Compassion?		
now you're	You really have	I don't know.	
just talking	to be a sick fuck		
nonsense.	to stab a three-		
	year-old kid and		
	then tell yourself	I'm just saying	
	that you're doing		
	it out of what?	All I'm trying to	
	Compassion? A	do is put myself	
	complete and	in his place.	
	utter fucking		
	whack job.	Maybe—when	
		he had his	
		breakdown—	
		maybe he	
		thought he was	
		protecting them	
		from the sepa-	
		ration. Maybe	
		he wanted—I	
		don't know—to	
	Look, if you	protect them	
	don't know,	from the pain	
	don't talk.	he was feeling?	
	Don't say		
	anything.		
Did he kill			
them, yes or no?			
		That's not the	
		question, Mom.	
		The question we	
		should be asking	

ELIZABETH:	JAMES:	DANIEL:	MELISSA:
		is, was he of sound mind?	
Oh anyone can say they're crazy!			
		He didn't choose to go crazy, Mom! It just happened, like it could happen to any one of us.	
No.	Bullshit.		Not me.
		One morning, he woke up and realized he killed his children.	
	Out of compassion?		
		But that's what insanity is: killing your kids and thinking you're doing it out of compassion!	
	So is it compassion that you're feeling when you take money from Mom?		
		Huh?	
James	I'm asking you if—Mom, please! I'm asking you if		

ELIZABETH:	JAMES:	DANIEL:	MELISSA:
	compassion		
	is what you		
	feel when you		
	steal money		
	from Mom?		
			James, we said
	Melissa! We're		we'd wait
	done pretend-		
	ing! We're		
	here to talk to		
	Daniel so we're		
	gonna talk		
	to him.	*(DANIEL gets up.)*	
	Daniel, sit down.		
		I'll get up if I	
		want to.	

The platform begins to rotate from the dining room to the living room.

ELIZABETH:	JAMES:	DANIEL:	MELISSA:
	(getting up)		
	Daniel, we want		
	you to stop		
	stealing money		
	from Mom.		
		Who the hell	
Daniel, please,		are you to lec-	
sit down.		ture me, huh?	
	Your brother.	*(DANIEL backs into*	
		the living room.)	No one wants
		My brother?	to lecture you,
	Yeah, your	Okay you're my	Daniel. We want
	brother.	brother. But I	you to be happy,
		don't need any	that's all.
		lessons from	

ELIZABETH:	**JAMES:**	**DANIEL:**	**MELISSA:**
(ELIZABETH walks toward the living room.)	*(JAMES walks toward the living room.)*	anyone, especially not from someone who went bankrupt.	*(MELISSA walks toward the living room.)*
	I never went bankrupt.	You did. You went bank-	*(to JAMES)*
Daniel, this isn't what this is about.		rupt. Yes, you went bankrupt!	When?
	No, Daniel, that's not true. I did not go bankrupt.	Summer 2003. I remember it very well! But you didn't actu-	
Daniel, we're not talking about James. We're talking about you!		ally go bankrupt because why . . . ? Because Daddy paid off all your debts! That's	
Daniel!	Okay, but	what's important here. Dad paid off twenty grand for you! So when	Danny
	I paid it back. I worked for him for five years and	I think about that, I have a really hard time	
This isn't the topic of this discussion.	I paid him back every single fucking cent that I owed him.	taking advice about how to live my life from someone who	
Stop comparing yourself, Daniel.		ran up a debt of twenty thousand dollars, okay?	
	I'm not trying to tell you how to live your life.		
	I don't care how	*(He laughs.)*	

ELIZABETH:	JAMES:	DANIEL:	MELISSA:
	you live your life.	Yeah right. You	
	All I want is for	don't care.	We all care about
	you to stop steal-	*(to MELISSA)*	you, Daniel.
	ing from Mom's	He doesn't care!	
James cares about	bank account—	*(to JAMES)*	
you, Daniel!	stop dipping into	I'm not steal-	
	it like it's a bowl	ing from her	
	of candy, you got	account.	He's not
	that? All she has		saying that to
	to live on is the		attack you.
	money she made	*(DANIEL goes into*	
	after she sold	*the living room.)*	
	the house, and I	I'm not stealing	
	don't want any of	from anyone's	
	that money used	account.	
	to pay off your		I believe you.
	fucking debts!		

JAMES, MELISSA, and ELIZABETH burst into the living room.

OLIVIA: Mom!

TYLER watches MELISSA's reaction. The adults don't pay attention to the children. The dialogue continues without interruption.

ELIZABETH:	JAMES:	DANIEL:	MELISSA:
		I'm not stealing	
		from anyone's	
		account.	*(to JAMES)*
			He's not steal-
			ing from her
	(to MELISSA)		account.
	What do you		
	mean he's not		
	stealing from		

ELIZABETH:	**JAMES:**	**DANIEL:**	**MELISSA:**
	her account? Mom, did Daniel take money from your account, yes or no?		
(ELIZABETH lowers her gaze.)			
	See! So let's stop saying he isn't stealing		
I transferred money into his account.	from her		
	What do you mean you transferred money into his account?		
Because I transferred money into his account.			
What did you want me to do? Let him sleep on	Mom!		
the streets? He's	Fuck, Mom!		
my son! I didn't			Okay, James,
even know how much debt he had! Poof—just like that—not a cent! I have no idea what he uses	Sure, let him stay here for a couple of weeks, that I can get, but paying off his debts? For fuck sakes!		could you stop swearing for a bit?
his credit card for. He must be		I told you I'll pay you back.	

ELIZABETH:	**JAMES:**	**DANIEL:**	**MELISSA:**
eating out in			
restaurants. I			
don't want you			
to pay me back,			
dear. I just want		I'm going to pay	
you to find a		you back.	
job, a job that			He'll pay
will make you			her back.
happy, and one	Don't you worry,		
that you can	he'll pay you back.	I'm going to	*(OLIVIA follows*
hold on to.			*MELISSA closely,*
		Stop saying	*tries to hold her*
	What does he	that, Mom! I	*hand.)*
	owe you? Ten	have a really big	
(to JAMES)	thousand?	interview next	
Oh more		week and I have	
than that.		lots of other	
	What?	projects. You	
Projects! It's easy	How much.	may not have	
to have proj-		noticed but I've	
ects! Especially	How much?	worked on lots	*(to ELIZABETH)*
when they never		of projects in	Don't say that,
work out. Oh		my life and lots	Mom! It's import-
really, which	How much does	more are in the	ant to have projects.
ones? Name one.	he owe you?	works.	*(to DANIEL)*
Name a single			Great, Daniel.
paying project?		*(to MELISSA)*	Which projects?
	(TYLER pretends to	Projects, Melissa,	
	get his claws out	projects!	
	and that he wants		Never mind, I
(to DANIEL)	*to eat OLIVIA.)*		was just asking.
Why don't you			
call your cousin		*(to ELIZABETH)*	
Luke? He's very		I knew you	
successful. I'm		were going to	

ELIZABETH:	**JAMES:**	**DANIEL:**	**MELISSA:**
sure he could help you find a job. But how do you know? You don't know, you haven't called him! What do you have to lose?	Mom, how much?	bring that up again. He's not looking for someone like me. I have too much experience for them.	*(to JAMES)* You know, James, Mom puts money in my account too sometimes.
Since when is experience such a bad thing for someone to have? I don't understand.	*(to MELISSA)* I know, Melissa, but you have a kid, it's not the same! So please stop defending him, it's not helping!	There's no point in calling him. They want kids fresh out of university who they'll be able to train.	
Do either of you understand that? I don't understand it.		And besides, Luke's father gave him his job, okay?	I don't think there's any point in attacking him either.
	I'm not attacking him.	He didn't have to do anything for it.	
		He's had it easy.	Sorry, but you're being very aggressive.
	Okay, whatever. *(to ELIZABETH)*	Meanwhile I have always made my own way.	
For once in your life, will you stop comparing yourself to other people, Daniel!	Mom Mom, how much does Daniel owe you?		
(to JAMES) I don't know.	Mom, how much?		
	What do you mean you don't know?		

ELIZABETH:	**JAMES:**	**DANIEL:**	**MELISSA:**
I stopped keeping track.			
	I bet you know what you owe her, don't you?		
		It's none of your business.	
	Yeah, clearly it's none of my business.	I said I'd pay her back and I'm going to pay her back, okay?	Okay, but still, we just want to make sure that
			We believe you, Dan.
	(to ELIZABETH*)* You know what you gave him this month	So from now on, I don't think I need to be accountable to	
	though, right?	anyone, espe-	No one
I don't know.	When you take money out with your card, you can see what withdrawals were made, can't you? Like	cially not to someone who took five years to pay off his debts. Thank you very much, Melissa, but	No one is holding you accountable. We just want to help you. I just want to help you, Daniel. Me.
Uh	what was it this month? / Mom?	I don't need any help.	Okay. Okay, never mind.

OLIVIA: Mom!

MELISSA doesn't react. The dialogue continues without interruption.

ELIZABETH:	**JAMES:**	**DANIEL:**	**MELISSA:**
			(to OLIVIA)
I don't know, I don't have my card.			Olivia, we're talking now. Go play in the park with your cousin.
	Why don't you have your card? Did you lose it?		
No.			
	Where's your card?		
	Mom, where's your card?		
Daniel has it.			
			What do you mean Daniel has your card?
I wanted him to run an errand for me, so I gave him my card.			
	Fuck!	I'll give it back any- time she wants. I didn't steal it! Here it is. The card. *(He puts his hand into his pocket.)* I'm not taking orders from you. She asked me to run some errands for her, okay? I'll give it back to her myself if that's okay!	Mom! You know Dan has a prob- lem with money. You can't give him your card like that, seri- ously! You're not helping. But he's not on the streets! You've been put- ting him up for six months!
All right, James, do me a favour and stop swearing. *(to MELISSA)* Oh, would you let your child live on the streets? No, I didn't think so. A mother will do anything for her child. Anything.	*(to DANIEL)* Give it. Dan, give me the card. Give it. Give me the card, Daniel! Okay.		

ELIZABETH:	JAMES:	DANIEL:	MELISSA:
	Give it back to her.		
		I'm giving it back to her.	
	Now.		

DANIEL holds the card out for ELIZABETH to take.

ELIZABETH:	JAMES:	DANIEL:	MELISSA:
Give it back to me later.			
	What do you mean, "later"?	Okay. *(DANIEL puts the card back in his pocket.)*	Mom!
Because I asked him to go get something for me, okay?			
			I'll go.
No, I don't want you to.		Okay, you saw this. It's not	
		me—she wants me to keep her	Why don't you want me to?
Daniel and I already talked about it.		card. So don't come to me later and accuse me of dipping into her account, because I'm not. I'm going to pay her	
(to DANIEL) I don't want you to pay me back.		back the money I borrowed. She gave me her card so I could get her groceries. But if anyone here	

ELIZABETH:	JAMES:	DANIEL:	MELISSA:
		wants to take my place, that's fine with me.	
			What do you mean?
		All I'm saying is that if I hadn't been here, who knows what would've happened.	
	What?		Like what?
Daniel, not now.		*(to ELIZABETH)* They're attack-ing me so I'm defending myself.	
	Am I missing something here?		
	You're leeching off your own mother and now	*(to JAMES)* I'm not leeching off anybody.	
	you're acting like you're the victim? Is that what's going on here? No one asked you for anything, bro, so stop whining to me about how much you're sacrificing		Daniel, like what?
James, that's enough. I think we get it.	for your mother while you're bleeding her dry		
	and stealing what	Bleeding her dry?	

ELIZABETH:	JAMES:	DANIEL:	MELISSA:
	little money she		
	has left! Yeah,		
	bleeding her dry!		
		If I hadn't been	
		here, Mom	
Boys, please!		wouldn't be alive	
		right now, okay?	
	What the hell		
	are you talking		
	about?		
		Mom fell.	
			When?
		Last month	
		Mom fell and	
I did not fall!		Yes, Mom, you	
		fell! And she	
		couldn't get back	
		up. I'm the one	
		who found her.	
		She'd been lying	
		on the floor for	
		three hours.	
			Three hours?
	Why the hell		
	didn't you tell me?		
It was nothing.			
I was picking	Nothing?		
something up and			
my back went out.			
		Your back didn't	
It's really not a		go out. You lost	
big deal.		your balance and	
		you fell.	
I did not fall.			

ELIZABETH:	JAMES:	DANIEL:	MELISSA:
	Did she fall or didn't she?		
			I thought I noticed you were limping.
Melissa, for crying out loud, I've always had a bit of a limp!			
	Mom, this isn't twenty questions, okay. Did you fall or not?		
Well I might have tripped			
	For fuck sakes! And you couldn't get up after?		
I had the wind knocked out of me.			
			For three hours?
Of course not for three hours. After that I rolled over on my back and I—I meditated. That's all.	*(to* DANIEL*)* Why didn't you call me?		
What should he call you for? To say what? What difference would it have made?		She didn't want me to call you.	*(to* DANIEL*)* You should have called us anyway.

ELIZABETH:	JAMES:	DANIEL:	MELISSA:
	The difference is we would've known.		
No one needs to know about this.			
			Mom, we're your kids! We should at least know when something happens to you.
"At least"			
I'm under no obligation to give you a detailed report every time I fall. Honestly, I'm a little offended!			
	"Every time"? So this wasn't the only time?		
No, dear, everybody falls!			
	Sure. But they're able to get back up after.		
(ELIZABETH walks around.) Look. I'm no worse for wear. I can walk, no problem!			
			Mom, no one's saying you can't walk!
(to MELISSA) Well they better not be! Look, I can even stand on one leg if you like.			

ELIZABETH:	**JAMES:**	**DANIEL:**	**MELISSA:**
(She stands on a leg.) Oh, well, I beg your pardon! But this is my house and I'll stand if I want to, thank you very much. Can you believe this guy?	Mom, sit down.		
	If I lose my balance and fall on the floor all I get is a bruise. It's different with you.		
I didn't even get a bruise!			
	This time.		
Wanna bet? Go on, push me! *(ELIZABETH pushes JAMES.)* Come on!			
	Mom.		What James is trying to say is that at your age there's a much higher risk of a serious fracture.
"At my age"! She's talking like I'm a hundred! I've fallen lots of times and I've never broken anything!			
	(to DANIEL) Lots of times?	*(to JAMES)* I didn't know.	*(to ELIZABETH)* When?

ELIZABETH:	**JAMES:**	**DANIEL:**	**MELISSA:**
This is none of your concern. I don't want to make a big deal about it! Can we just— Why are you so obsessed with me falling?	*(to* ELIZABETH*)* But, Mom, do you hear what you're saying?	*(to* MELISSA*)* This is news to me.	How many times? How many— Mom, how many times did you fall?
			We're not. We just want you to be safe!
I'm doing just fine here.			
	It could have been way worse.		
Well it wasn't.			
			You can't keep living here on your own.
But I wasn't alone! Thank goodness Daniel was here! Not everyone can count on their children these days! Honestly, I have nothing to complain about.			

OLIVIA: Mom! Mom!

MELISSA: / Olivia, not now!

ELIZABETH:	**JAMES:**	**DANIEL:**	**MELISSA:**
			Daniel can't keep living here, Mom. It's not good for you. It's not good for him. Daniel needs to get his act together and he's the only one who can do that.
Yeah, but in the meantime, while he sorts things out			
			No, not "in the meantime." This is happening right now. But if you need help here at home, we'll call LHS.
	(JAMES follows DANIEL.)	*(DANIEL goes back to the dining room.)*	
	Where you going?		
		Wherever I want.	
I don't need help! And forget LHS. I'm not disabled enough for them.			
	You're staying here.		
		Who do you think you are?	
	Your brother.		
			Okay then we'll pay for someone to come.
		My brother?	
	Yeah, your brother.		
Do you have any idea how much a private nurse costs? An arm and a leg, Melissa!		You really like saying that.	
	Because you seem to forget it.		
			It's not that expensive. I don't mean a nurse who's here twenty-four hours a day. I'm just
		Just because we both spent nine months in the same womb doesn't mean you can talk to	

ELIZABETH:	**JAMES:**	**DANIEL:**	**MELISSA:**
Even still. Don't		me like this. A	talking about
try and tell me		brother wouldn't	someone who
that doesn't cost		act the way you're	comes by once
anything either.		acting now.	in a while.
I don't need it.	Are you seriously		
	so delusional		Then what's
	that you think		going to happen
	you're actually		if you fall again?
Someone will end	doing a good		
up finding me.	deed every time		
Daniel found me.	you milk her		
	for cash?		Daniel isn't a
He's a natural		I take care of	health-care
caregiver, in case		my mother	professional,
you didn't know.		much more	Mom. He's not
		than you do,	qualified to take
		okay? I was	care of you. I'm
		here when she	sure he is, but
		needed me.	now Daniel has
	I've heard		to stop living
	enough. Give		off his mother
	me back		and finally
	her card.		start living his
		I'll give it back	own life!
		to her myself.	

DANIEL takes the card out.

ELIZABETH:	**JAMES:**	**DANIEL:**	**MELISSA:**
		Look, I know	
		what you all	
		think of me,	
		okay? You think	
		that I've wasted	
		my life, but I	

ELIZABETH:	**JAMES:**	**DANIEL:**	**MELISSA:**
		haven't wasted	
		my life, okay?	
		I know that. I	
		had dreams and	No one said you
		I followed those	wasted your life,
		dreams, okay?	Daniel!
		(DANIEL cries.)	And you
		I didn't wait	achieved them
		around for	too—no one's
		someone to help	saying you didn't!
		me. I started	
		my own law	
		practice, I ini-	
		tiated projects,	
		I developed all	
		kinds of skills,	
		I travelled all	
		over the world.	
	Then why can't	I don't think	
	you hold down	anyone here can	
	a job for longer	say that!	
	than two weeks?	*(DANIEL laughs.)*	
		What! I've held	
		down a job for	
		longer than two	
	Well, I can't	weeks! I can	
	remember the	send you my cv	
	last time. You	if you want to	
	know what your	see it.	
	problem is?		
	Pride, man, pride!		
	No job is good		
	enough for you!		
	Now give the card		
	to me. Give it!		

JAMES tries to take the card from DANIEL. DANIEL retreats.

ELIZABETH:	JAMES:	DANIEL:	MELISSA:
	Daniel, give me the card.		
		It's not your card.	
			Well it's not yours either.
		I never said it was my card.	
	Well, give it back to her then.		
(to JAMES) I'm old enough to get it back myself, thank you very much.		I'll give it back to her when she asks me to give it back to her.	
Give me back my card, Daniel.			
		You don't want me to do your shopping anymore?	
I'll do it myself.			
		The elevator's broken.	
I know.			
I'm perfectly aware of the situation.		You'll have to climb three flights of stairs, up and down.	
	I can do your shopping for you		I'll go later, if you let me
I'm big girl, I can do my own			

ELIZABETH:	**JAMES:**	**DANIEL:**	**MELISSA:**
shopping! Now give me back my card.			
		Why? You're afraid I'll empty your account?	
I'm not afraid you'll empty my account. I just want to have my card back.		*(DANIEL backs away toward the balcony.)*	
(ELIZABETH walks toward the balcony.) *(to MELISSA)* I don't need in-home care! Will you stop with that nonsense? *(to DANIEL)* I wanted to help you out of a rough	*(JAMES walks toward the balcony.)* *(to DANIEL)* Oh that's fucking rich! You want me to tell you what happened? You decided you wanted to take it easy and screw everyone else! You don't give a shit if she has money for rent. You take. You fucking take and take as if the world owes you something. And	You're afraid I'll empty your account when you know I never took a cent from you! All I ever did was help you! I did your shopping because you couldn't walk! I always gave you back the exact change, with the receipt! The only money I got was the money you insisted on giving me! You're the one who deposited money into my account! So it's very hard for me when I'm being	*(MELISSA walks toward the balcony.)* *(to DANIEL)* If you hadn't taken all that money from her, Mom would be able to pay for the in-home care that she needs now. She'd be able to live out the rest of her life without having to worry about

ELIZABETH:	JAMES:	DANIEL:	MELISSA:
patch, Daniel, but I think I made things worse. No one here's attacking you, Daniel, honestly! No one's on trial, Daniel! No one's judging you! Only you know what you've done! Give it, Danny.	fuck everyone else. You stuff your fucking pockets while everyone else is struggling to make it to the end of the month. You know what? You're a cold-blooded bastard. I'd be fucking ashamed if I were you. Give me the card. Okay, that's enough of this shit.	attacked like— Like I'm some sort of low-life criminal. The lowest of the low, judged, sentenced, and, and, and ordered to give back something I absolutely did not steal! And if you're both feeling guilty because you weren't there for your mother when she needed you, that's not my problem. I'm not your punching bag!	money. I'm sorry, Daniel, but no one forced you to accept that money! We love you, Daniel! We just want what's best for you! But no one's going to do it for you. We just need you to show us that you want to make it on your own! So please give her back the card. Daniel, give it.

JAMES tries to take the card from DANIEL. They wrestle. The platform begins to rotate, from the living room to the balcony. JAMES pins DANIEL against the bookcase. Books fall.

MELISSA: The bookcase!

ELIZABETH: / Boys, stop it! You're going to break something!

Their wrestling moves onto the balcony. JAMES *takes* DANIEL *down. Everyone goes onto the balcony.*

Stop it, you're going to / get hurt!

OLIVIA: Mom!

JAMES *pins* DANIEL *to the ground.* MELISSA *pushes* OLIVIA *and* TYLER *into the living room and shuts the sliding doors.*

DANIEL: Do you see yourself right now?

JAMES: The only one responsible for what's happening here, Dan, is you!

DANIEL *stops resisting.* JAMES *takes the card out of* DANIEL*'s pocket and gets up.* JAMES *hands* ELIZABETH *the card.* DANIEL *gets up.* JAMES *and* DANIEL *catch their breath.*

OLIVIA: *(from living room)* Mom!

MELISSA: What.

MELISSA *opens the sliding doors.* OLIVIA *glances at* TYLER.

What?

OLIVIA *comes onto the balcony.*

Olivia, what is it?

OLIVIA: Tyler killed a squirrel.

MELISSA: What?

OLIVIA: There was a squirrel on the balcony and Tyler used a broom and hit the squirrel and knocked it off the balcony.

MELISSA: I don't understand—when was this?

OLIVIA: Before.

MELISSA: Tyler, is this true?

Pause.

JAMES: Tyler?

Pause.

Answer.

TYLER: *(at balcony door)* Yes.

Pause.

MELISSA: Darling, squirrels are very dangerous. They might look friendly, but under their little furry coat, squirrels are just rats. They eat garbage. They dig through the trash. They could have rabies. If that squirrel had bitten you, you would've gotten very sick. Tyler did a good thing knocking the squirrel off the balcony. Squirrels are vermin.

Pause.

ELIZABETH: Okay, go back inside now, Olivia. Go have some ice cream.

OLIVIA goes into the apartment and disappears. TYLER goes into the dining room. Pause.

JAMES: You need to move out. You can't keep living here at Mom's.

Pause.

MELISSA: Is there a friend you could stay with until you find a job?

DANIEL: No.

MELISSA: Your old buddy from high school—Jim?

DANIEL: I haven't seen him in ten years.

JAMES: Where are you going to go?

DANIEL: I don't know.

Pause.

JAMES: You could come stay at my place if you want. I know Bowmanville isn't exactly next door, but I have a job for you, / a bed, three meals a day

DANIEL: Thanks, I'll manage.

JAMES: Where will you go?

DANIEL: I don't know.

Pause.

JAMES: Melissa, do you have room at your place?

Pause.

Melissa?

MELISSA: Uh, I'd have to check with Philip, but yeah, we have an empty room, sure. Absolutely.

DANIEL: Thanks, Melissa. I'll manage.

MELISSA: Well if you ever—

Pause. MELISSA *goes inside.*

ELIZABETH: Go back inside, boys. It's going to rain.

ELIZABETH *goes back into the apartment. Pause.* JAMES *holds his hand out for* DANIEL *to shake.* DANIEL *leaves him hanging.* JAMES *goes into the apartment.* DANIEL *stays on the balcony, alone.*

ACT 3

1

The platform rotates from the balcony to the dining room. Everyone is seated around the table. OLIVIA *looks at them as if they're strange and unusual sculptures.*

2

One year later. Dining room. ELIZABETH, JAMES, TYLER, DANIEL, SUZIE,* *and* MELISSA *are seated around the table covered with plates, food, and wine glasses. They've all just finished their meal, except* DANIEL, *who is still eating.*

OLIVIA *runs over to her mother.* SUZIE *grabs hold of her as she passes.*

SUZIE:	ELIZABETH:	JAMES:	TYLER:	MELISSA:
Well aren't you just the cutest! Isn't she just the cutest? She is so cute! Little arms, little nose,				

* Suzie's ethnicity can be adapted to suit casting.

SUZIE:	ELIZABETH:	JAMES:	TYLER:	MELISSA:
little dress,				
goddamn				
she is cute!				Her name is
Olivia!				Olivia.
That's right,				
I know your				
name. How				
about that?				
I know your				
name. Yeah.				
I know lots				
of other stuff				
about you,				
too. I asked				
Daniel all				
about you.				
How old are				
you, sweetie?				
				Eleven.
Eleven?				
Well, then				
you're a big				
girl now.				
So that				
means you're				
in what?				
Grade five?				
				Grade six
Grade six,				
of course.				
Then you're				
old enough				
to answer all				
by yourself.				
You don't				

SUZIE:	ELIZABETH:	JAMES:	TYLER:	MELISSA:
need your mommy to answer for you, do ya?				
				She's just being shy.
Oh well. We'll just have to get to know each other better. How about you come over here some-time? I could babysit you. Would you like me to babysit you?				
Huh?				
Me and Daniel could babysit you. What do you say, huh, Daniel?				

DANIEL eats.

SUZIE:	ELIZABETH:	JAMES:	OLIVIA:	MELISSA:
There's no talking to				

SUZIE:	ELIZABETH:	JAMES:	OLIVIA:	MELISSA:
him when he's eating.				
		Dan is very polite. He doesn't talk with his mouth full.		
Good manners, yeah. Well lemme tell ya, sometimes it can take a long, long time.				
				It's important to chew your food properly. People don't chew their food enough
Oh boy, he sure chews all right, that's for sure. I've never seen anyone eat slow like that. I'm telling you, sometimes by the time I go to bed, he hasn't even made it to dessert yet. Liz, I don't know what				

SUZIE:	ELIZABETH:	JAMES:	OLIVIA:	MELISSA:
you fed him when he was little that made him so scared of gagging. *(to OLIVIA)* Do you want some dessert, sweetie?				
				Dessert doesn't exist in our house.
Well you're not at your house now. You can have dessert. How about some, jeez I dunno, some ice cream?				We don't call it dessert. We call it a "meal com-plement." She can have a piece of fruit if she likes.
Fruit? Not a lot of choice there. Your uncle only bought bananas. *(SUZIE imitates a monkey.)* You want bananas?				

SUZIE:	ELIZABETH:	JAMES:	OLIVIA:	MELISSA:
Yeah?				One banana.
Which one you want?			*(pointing at a banana)* May I please have that one?	
"May I." Well! Where'd she get that from? She talks like a book! "May I"! I sure didn't talk like that when I was eleven. "May I," "May I please"!				

TYLER gets up.

SUZIE:	ELIZABETH:	JAMES:	TYLER:	MELISSA:
			Can I go now?	
		No. When you're invited over for dinner, you sit and you talk after.		
			(TYLER sits.) But it's boring!	
Yeah it is boring. You are so right.				

SUZIE:	**ELIZABETH:**	**JAMES:**	**TYLER:**	**MELISSA:**
When I was your age, I thought adult conversations were boring too. So, so boring! I liked chasing after boys in the park way more.				
			Oh, really?	
		Tyler, do that one more time— one more!		
Well he isn't just gorgeous, he's a smart-ass to boot! I like it! He's no pushover! I like it!				
		(to SUZIE*)* Yeah, well, he's a smart-ass, that's for sure.	*(*TYLER *gets up.)*	
		(to TYLER*)* Not if you ask like that.	Can I go now?	
			"May I please be excused?"	

SUZIE:	ELIZABETH:	JAMES:	TYLER:	MELISSA:
		I told you: there's more to being polite than words. It's your tone too. Sit down. Be interested. And join the conversation.		

TYLER sits, exasperated.

SUZIE:	ELIZABETH:	JAMES:	DANIEL:	MELISSA:
	You must have a lot on your plate, looking after your grandmother.			
Oh I haven't looked after my grand-mother for a while now.				
	Oh really? Daniel didn't tell me			
Get this, Liz. It's a Friday night, right? I'm totally beat. I get home,	that you			

SUZIE:	ELIZABETH:	JAMES:	DANIEL:	MELISSA:
must be				
ten o'clock,				
I hear this				
noise—like a				
little whine.				
Coming				
from her				
room. I open				
the door, and				
Pierre's there				
at the foot				
of the bed				
shaking, ya				
know, whim-				
pering. Then		Pierre?		
I see this			Her grand-	
big puddle			mother's dog.	
coming				
from the				
bathroom,				
and then I				
see the tips				
of her toes				
poking out,				
and I say to				
her, "Granny,				
what's goin'				
on in there?"				
She says,				
"As you can				
very well				
see, I fell				
down!" She's				
clearly had				
a few. So I				

SUZIE:	**ELIZABETH:**	**JAMES:**	**DANIEL:**	**MELISSA:**
say, “Granny, this is crazy, you can’t be				
boozing like		Pierre?		
this.” And			A Maltese.	
she says to me, “Mind your own business.” Whoa. I say, “It is my business, since I’m the one who’s got to pick you up.” Then she starts swearing and yelling at me, so I grab my phone and I say, “Listen, you old bag, just keep your trap shut until the ambulance gets here.” She says, “Don’t call the ambulance.” I say, “What? You				

SUZIE:	ELIZABETH:	JAMES:	DANIEL:	MELISSA:
want me to carry you to the hospital on my back?" She says, "Give me my face cream." "Your face cream?" She says, "I don't want them to see me like this." She wanted to get herself all dolled up before the paramedics got there! *(SUZIE laughs.)*	Your grand-mother must be a very ele-gant woman.			
And were they ever handsome. Oh man! I mean these guys were total hunks! Makes you ask yourself, "Why didn't I become a nurse?" Anyhoo. When they				

SUZIE:	ELIZABETH:	JAMES:	DANIEL:	MELISSA:
put her on the stretcher, she starts playing the martyr, "Oh, thank you, you saved my life." Like I didn't do anything for her and forced her to stew in her own shit! *(SUZIE laughs.)* So then I say to the guys, "I'll go with you." She says, "There's no room in the ambulance." "What do you mean there's no room?" "There's not enough room for you." I say, "Trust me. There's room." So				

SUZIE:	ELIZABETH:	JAMES:	DANIEL:	MELISSA:
she says, "Well there might be room for you, but not your fat ass."				
Right?!		*(JAMES laughs.)*		
(SUZIE laughs.)		Yeah, she sounds like a real piece of work.		
What an old bitch!				
		Has she met Daniel yet?		
Are you kidding me!? She loves him. "Oh, Daniel . . . Oh, my sweet, darling Daniel . . . " Anything to smooch him and drive me nuts.				
(SUZIE laughs.)	It mustn't have been easy for your grandmother to adapt to life here in Canada.	*(JAMES laughs.)*		
Oh my grandmother fit right in,				

SUZIE:	ELIZABETH:	JAMES:	DANIEL:	MELISSA:
Liz. She married a true-blue hoser, walked all over him his whole life, watched every single episode of *All My Children*, and she's got an even worse mouth on her than me. So no, she didn't have any trouble adapting to life here. She plays the poor old immigrant lady when it suits her! "People here are racist! People here are ignorant! People here are so rude!" I say to her, "I don't want				

SUZIE:	ELIZABETH:	JAMES:	DANIEL:	MELISSA:
to generalize, but the last guy I met was a total moron. He got so drunk he puked all over my shoes, and that was before he tried to kiss me. And you know what? Like it or not, Granny, you're Canadian." She says, "I'm not Canadian. I'm Polish!" "Well if you're Polish, then why don't you go back there and sleep it off!" Yeah! I'm a third-generation Canadian, and I'm not afraid to say				

SUZIE:	**ELIZABETH:**	**JAMES:**	**DANIEL:**	**MELISSA:**
it: immigrants who don't want to adapt don't belong here. 'Cause I know 'em, eh? I've heard everything, all that victim talk! Well I only have one thing to say: go ahead. Wear your turban or burka at home if you want, but don't walk down King Street with it on! Right?! And I don't think there's anything intolerant about that. Besides, they're the intolerant ones. They come over here with				

SUZIE:	ELIZABETH:	JAMES:	DANIEL:	MELISSA:
their chauvinist and sexist culture, chain their women to the stove, and we're not supposed to say anything about it? I mean, come on! Right?!				
	It's very decent of you to have taken care of your grandmother all these years.			
Yeah, well after her stint in the hospital, I said, "I've been taking care of her for two years. I love her even if she's a hateful old cow. She might be my grandmother, but enough is enough, you				

SUZIE:	ELIZABETH:	JAMES:	DANIEL:	MELISSA:
know?" So I sat both my mother and grandmother down on the same couch, which is already something. Barely three seconds go by before they're at each other's throats. Then I said, "All right, shut up and listen. You—you're going to stop lying to the lady from social services about how you can take care of yourself, because ya can't. And you, you need to step up and be her daughter and find a decent				

SUZIE:	**ELIZABETH:**	**JAMES:**	**DANIEL:**	**MELISSA:**
place for your mother. Because I don't have either the skills or capacity to keep taking care of you. 'Cause if you're not in a home by tomorrow morning, I'm checking myself into CAMH, stat." *(SUZIE laughs.)* I was totally losing it! "If it's between you and me, sorry, but I gotta choose me." Then she starts crying, "You're abandoning me! How could you be so selfish?!" Yeah, that's right. Do				

SUZIE:	ELIZABETH:	JAMES:	DANIEL:	MELISSA:
I look like a saint to you? Do I have a hello floating over my head?				
			A halo	
What?				
			A halo	
Hello, halo! Everybody here under-stands what I mean, right?				
		Totally		
			Except it's halo.	
	Daniel, it's not polite to correct people in public.			
			I'll correct people if I want to, okay?	
He's sure something else, isn't he? He always has to be right.				
				Daniel never makes mistakes.
Like my boss. The				

SUZIE:	**ELIZABETH:**	**JAMES:**	**DANIEL:**	**MELISSA:**
other day, I go into her office. And I say, "Esther, are you on the network?" She says, "Yes, I'm connected." I say, "So you're able to go on the Internet?" She says, "Yes, I am." "So you're getting my emails, right?" "Yes, I'm receiving your emails." "Well how about you answer them since we work here together?" So then she looks at me, "I'm getting your emails, but I can't read them." So I say,				

SUZIE:	**ELIZABETH:**	**JAMES:**	**DANIEL:**	**MELISSA:**
"Well if the font's too small make the window bigger or buy some glasses." She says, "The problem isn't that it's too small. The problem is that they're not written in English." Oh, yeah, okay! What are they written in then? Greek? She says, "There's too many mistakes, I can't read them." I mean, wake up! This is 2022! No one's got time to write airy fairy poems, so open your inbox, click on				

SUZIE:	**ELIZABETH:**	**JAMES:**	**DANIEL:**	**MELISSA:**
my emails, and hit reply, stat! *(SUZIE laughs.)*				

OLIVIA tries to get away. SUZIE keeps her there.

SUZIE:	**ELIZABETH:**	**JAMES:**	**TYLER:**	**MELISSA:**
			Yeah, that's like my dad. I'm going to this show with my buds. Then before I leave, he says, "Call me when you get there." And I say, "Okay," but like, it's dumb, no one ever calls their dad, you know.	
		You said you were going to call me.		
			So I send him a text, to let him know I'm not dead,	
		What he wrote was, "Imntded. Cyal8r."	right, then, and after that, well, I go to the	

SUZIE:	ELIZABETH:	JAMES:	TYLER:	MELISSA:
		That's it.	show. Then I get home.	
		At two in the morning.	He's all, "Blah blah blah, you didn't call me, you can't be trusted, blah blah blah." I say, "Dad, didn't you get my text?" And he says, "Yeah but a text isn't the same as calling. You were supposed to call." Come on, the entire planet is texting and you want us to talk?	
		Exactly.		
			The music was too loud, we wouldn't've even been able to talk.	
		You could've gone outside.		

SUZIE:	ELIZABETH:	JAMES:	TYLER:	MELISSA:
			And not seen the show, you mean.	
What show was it?				
			Fred Penner.	
Fred Penner? He does concerts?				
		He's joking.	You know, he bought me a phone so we can communicate, so I'm communicating.	He does concerts.
	The telephone was invented so people could talk to each other, did you know that?			
		Thanks, Mom.		
			Yeah but, Gramma, my phone can do stuff that's much more— advanced than just talking.	
		Like what? Shutting up?		
		(JAMES laughs.)	No, like writing texts,	

SUZIE:	ELIZABETH:	JAMES:	TYLER:	MELISSA:
			or getting them, or watching videos, or going online, or doing	
		Okay, Tyler, everyone knows what a smartphone is.	all kinds of stuff a regular phone can't do. If you actually knew what it was, you wouldn't say "smartphone."	
		Oh no? What would I say? An iPhone 20?		
			What are you talking about, Dad? The 15 isn't even out yet.	
		Okay, go to the living room, you're getting on my nerves.		
			Okay.	

OLIVIA watches TYLER exit, enviously.

SUZIE:	ELIZABETH:	JAMES:	DANIEL:	MELISSA:
	Suzanne			
Suzie. Call me Suzie				
	What's your position exactly?			
On what?				
	You were speak-ing about your job.			
What was I saying? Oh yeah, my boss! Yeah, no, I mean some people have no shame, right? They always want to tell you what to do. Well she might be my boss, but I don't answer to her or anyone else. Except my clients. And my clients are very happy with the service				

SUZIE:	ELIZABETH:	JAMES:	DANIEL:	MELISSA:
I provide. So if you're not happy with me, complain to my union. And then you'll find out pretty fast that our contract *(hits herself)* is rock solid.				
				We're lucky we have unions.
Sorry?				
				I'm saying that union members like us are actu-ally pretty
Excuse me?				lucky to have unions to defend us when
Unions? Are you serious?! Our union's a joke! I don't know how many times I had to fight with the union				

SUZIE:	ELIZABETH:	JAMES:	DANIEL:	MELISSA:
to make sure my rights were respected. Unions only care about one thing: protecting the interests of the union. But no one's going to pull anything on me. No way! You can count on that! Believe you me!				
		Oh! I believe you!		
Oh, you better!				

DANIEL has now finished what was on his plate. SUZIE and JAMES laugh. ELIZABETH gets up.

SUZIE:	ELIZABETH:	JAMES:	DANIEL:	MELISSA:
Hey, Liz, what are you doing?				
	I'm just going to clear a few things	Mom		Mom, come on, don't.
No way! Tonight you				

SUZIE:	ELIZABETH:	JAMES:	DANIEL:	MELISSA:
stay put, you	Olivia, go			
got that?	get me my			
You waited		Ma		
on everyone				Sit down
your whole				
life! It's your				
turn now!				

SUZIE gathers the plates. ELIZABETH sits back down.

SUZIE:	ELIZABETH:	JAMES:	DANIEL:	MELISSA:
	Daniel, don't		*(DANIEL pours*	
	let her clear		*himself a*	
	the table. I		*drink.)*	
Look, Daniel's	don't want			
going to	her doing			
finish chew-	the dishes!			
ing and I'm	I don't want			
going to do	her to. Do			
the dishes. No	you hear me?			
arguments. So				
just sit back	Daniel!			
and enjoy! I'm				
a very tradi-				
tional woman.				

SUZIE goes to the kitchen. OLIVIA takes refuge in MELISSA's arms.

SUZIE:	ELIZABETH:	JAMES:	DANIEL:	MELISSA:
(from kitchen)				
I'm telling				
you, Liz, your				
son doesn't				
know how				
lucky he is.				

SUZIE:	ELIZABETH:	JAMES:	DANIEL:	MELISSA:
(to DANIEL) When are you going to realize that I'm the woman of your dreams? *(coming into dining room)* Marry me already! He doesn't want to marry me.				
			You're already married.	
Yeah, that's right, always with the excuses.				
			I can't marry a married woman. It's against the law	
Oh come off it! I've been separated for ten years already!				
			Separated. Not divorced.	
Funny, isn't it? He won't marry me, but he has				

SUZIE:	ELIZABETH:	JAMES:	DANIEL:	MELISSA:
no problem sleeping with me.				
			Living in sin becomes me.	
Just admit that you're too much of a pussy to ask me to marry you.				
			I can't really do much without proof of divorce.	
Oh, don't you worry, I'll get those divorce papers. The other dum-my's gonna sign 'em sooner or later.				
			That could take a while.	
Give me six months.				
			It could take longer than six months, with all the proceedings. Okay. Six months.	
Wait Wait Six months!				

SUZIE:	**ELIZABETH:**	**JAMES:**	**DANIEL:**	**MELISSA:**
If you haven't asked me to marry you in six months, I'm kicking you out, you got that?				
(SUZIE laughs.)			We'll talk about it in six months.	
I mean, a girl can only let herself be strung along for so long, right?				
				I think it's beautiful when a woman asks a man to marry her.
Who, me?				
				Yes.
There's no way.				
				Oh I thought that
I'm never going to ask him to marry me.				
				Oh no?

SUZIE:	ELIZABETH:	JAMES:	DANIEL:	MELISSA:
Are you nuts? He's the one who's going to ask me to marry him, and it's gonna be a big wedding, too! An engagement ring, the knee on the ground, a big fancy restaurant, the works! *(to* DANIEL*)* Not Boston Pizza, okay. *(to everyone)* A big fancy restaurant on a beach somewhere.				
		Better start saving, Dan.		
You better believe it because this wedding's going to cost a pretty penny.				
		I bet.		

SUZIE:	ELIZABETH:	JAMES:	DANIEL:	MELISSA:
But you know I'm not the one with expensive tastes, eh.				
		Oh no?		
You know what he said to me the other day?				
		No I don't.		
He's sitting there, eating his toast, not saying a word, being a sourpuss as usual, and I say to him, "What's the matter?" He says, "Oh nothing." I say, "Listen, you, we're a couple. And couples talk to each other." He says, "I didn't sleep well." I say, "Okay." He says, "You take				

SUZIE:	ELIZABETH:	JAMES:	DANIEL:	MELISSA:
up the bed." Mister here thinks I take up too much room in bed! I say, "Hey, pal, if you're not happy, find yourself another girlfriend!" Honestly! Obviously he thinks it's cramped—he's been sleeping alone for forty-five years! He lies on his back, get this, arms and legs spread out wide. And I'm all scrunched up on the other side. Lucky for me I haven't hit the deck yet. *(She laughs.)*				

SUZIE:	ELIZABETH:	JAMES:	DANIEL:	MELISSA:
Then I say, "Okay. What do you think about a king-sized bed?" He says, "Good idea." So we head over to Sleep Country, try out a couple of beds, and then mister here chooses one. We get to the cash and the salesman asks, "How would you like to pay?" I say, "Ask him, it's his bed. He's the one paying." *(She laughs.)* You shoulda seen his face! Worth a thousand bucks, I tell ya! Two thousand				

SUZIE:	ELIZABETH:	JAMES:	DANIEL:	MELISSA:
three hundred and fifty seven, actually. *(to* ELIZABETH*)* I'm telling ya, Liz, this one was spoiled rotten. A regular little prince. *(*SUZIE *hits* DANIEL.*)* Marry me already! *(to* MELISSA*)* Don't you worry, he's gonna ask me sooner or later.				

SUZIE *sits at the table.*

JAMES: So, Dan? How's work going?

DANIEL: Fine. I'm finishing up a project.

MELISSA: Didn't you have an interview at a big firm?

DANIEL: Mm-hmm.

MELISSA: Have you heard anything?

DANIEL: Yes.

JAMES: And?

DANIEL: They called back.

MELISSA: Great.

DANIEL: They want me to take a test.

ELIZABETH: What kind?

DANIEL: It's just a psychometric test. If everything goes well, I start next week.

SUZIE:	ELIZABETH:	JAMES:	DANIEL:	MELISSA:
I found it	Make sure	Awesome!	It's not	Oh I'm so
for him, you	you study for	*(He applauds.)*	a done	happy. I'm
know. He	it. Or take a	Well done,	deal but	really happy
didn't want to	practice test	Dan. We		for you,
call. I say, "I'm	before. Or	believe in	Thanks.	brother!
gonna call if	talk to some-	you. You		Wow! This
you don't."	one who's	got this.	It's not that	is really
(She laughs.)	already taken	Let's have	kind of	good news!
Boy, was he	it. You need	a toast. Ma,	test, Mom.	
ever scared	to prepare	your glass.		
I'd do it!	for it.	Ma. To	Okay, fine.	
He called.	*(to JAMES)*	your job,		
Cheers.	Just a splash.	Daniel.		To work!

They drink.

SUZIE:	ELIZABETH:	JAMES:	DANIEL:	MELISSA:
We won't				
say no to				
a second				

SUZIE:	ELIZABETH:	JAMES:	DANIEL:	MELISSA:
paycheque,				
especially				
with all the				
changes				
we want				
to make				
around here.				
		What		
		changes?		
Didn't Daniel				
tell you guys?				
I'm moving				
in with him!			*(to JAMES)*	
Well, I totally		Oh! I get	I was going	
thought he		it. That's	to tell you.	
told you.		what all the		Well, I knew
That's actu-		marriage talk	I thought	about it.
ally kind of		was about.	I told	
why you're all		Well good	you guys.	
over here.		for you!		

Everyone drinks except ELIZABETH.

SUZIE:	ELIZABETH:	JAMES:	DANIEL:	MELISSA:
Yeah, no, it'll				
be good once				
it gets cleared				
out. Besides,				
Liz, you must				
want your				
furniture				
back, right?				
	I don't have			
	room for my			
	furniture.			

SUZIE:	ELIZABETH:	JAMES:	DANIEL:	MELISSA:
				Your books at least.
	I don't have room for my books either.			
				I'll put some shelves up on the wall.
	I don't think I'm allowed to drill holes in the wall.			
		It's your home, Mom. You can do whatever you want.	Sure you are. There's no reason you can't.	
	I won't be able to bring all my books there anyway.			
				Maybe not all of them, but at least a few. I'll pack them into boxes for you after. You
	I've already read them. I don't need them anymore. Everything I need is at the home:			can tell me which ones you want to keep.

SUZIE:	ELIZABETH:	JAMES:	DANIEL:	MELISSA:
	a library, a			
	variety store,			
	a hairdresser.			
You're right,	You can			
Liz. Nursing	keep them.			
homes now				I don't
are nothing				have room
like they were				for them.
in the olden	Then give			
days! Look at	them away.			
my granny:				I'm not
she basically				gonna just get
has a gym				rid of your
all to herself,				books, Ma.
with this	Sell them			
cute personal	to a used			
trainer who	bookstore.			
looks like a				Daniel,
Greek god,				couldn't you
and a sauna,				keep them?
and a steam			Aren't you	
room. Oh,			taking the	
man! You			bookcase?	
should see the				Yeah, the
showers at				bookcase. But
my gym! Ew!	*(to OLIVIA)*			not the books.
	Olivia, go		I can't keep all	
	and fetch me		those books.	
	my walker,		I don't have	
	will you,		the room.	
	kitten?		Speaking of,	
	(OLIVIA goes.)		when are you	
			coming to get	
		Where you	the bookcase	
		going?	anyway?	

SUZIE:	ELIZABETH:	JAMES:	DANIEL:	MELISSA:
	To get some air.			I thought you could keep it for a little bit longer.
Wait, I'm gonna help you.				
	Thank you very much but I'll manage.			
			Melissa, I just bought a bed and the movers are coming with Suzie's stuff tomorrow. Where do you expect me to put it?	
	(OLIVIA enters with the folded walker.)			Tomorrow? There's no way I'm going to be able to find someone to move a huge bookcase like that by tomorrow! I didn't know Suzie was moving in tomorrow!
	Okay, now open it like this.			
			You haven't called anyone yet?	
	(to OLIVIA) Turn it around. Bring it over. *(OLIVIA brings the walker over to ELIZABETH.)*			
Take my arm, Liz.	I need to be able to get up on my own, or my physiotherapist isn't		Well, if you don't come get the bookcase, I'm going to take it apart and put it	

SUZIE:	ELIZABETH:	JAMES:	DANIEL:	MELISSA:
	going to be happy.		out in the garbage.	
Come on, Daniel! We can just keep it. I like bookcases. They're nice. Instead of books maybe we could put my figurines on it?	*(*ELIZABETH *gets closer to her walker.)*			Are you insane? That bookcase belonged to our grand-mother. Mom gave
	I'm not supposed to pull. I have to push.		If it really meant so much to you, you would have figured out how to move it by now.	it to me, and I'm going to leave that bookcase to my daughter when I die! You can't just throw it out!
	Like this. *(She gets up with difficulty.)*	Maybe we could try selling it or something?		Sell it?
I'll go with you, Liz.	See? Not bad, huh?		That still doesn't solve who's going to move it.	Mom didn't give me her bookcase for me to turn
	No need. Thank you. *(She takes a few steps.)*	Whoever buys it will have to move it.		around and sell it! We're not talking about some
	(to OLIVIA*)* Come on now. We'll let the adults argue.	We just have to sell it for cheap.	Right. How much?	crappy IKEA bookcase. We're talking about a family heir-loom here!

SUZIE catches OLIVIA by the waist.

SUZIE:	ELIZABETH:	JAMES:	DANIEL:	MELISSA:
Hold on a minute, you! I didn't give you your banana yet! *(pointing at the bananas)* So? D'ya want a banana or not? You're not gonna tell me? You too shy, is that it? You wanna whisper it in my ear? *(She leans over to listen. OLIVIA bites her.)* Ow!				
				(MELISSA grabs OLIVIA by the arm.) Hey! What did you just do?
I think she bit me. But don't worry about it. It's no big deal.	Jesus	She really bit you?		Since when do you bite people?

SUZIE:	ELIZABETH:	JAMES:	DANIEL:	MELISSA:
			Show me.	
It's not bleeding.				
It's It's It's It's nothing, it's just a little bite. It's nothing.			I can see the bite mark.	
(She laughs.)	Hold on, I'll go and get you a washcloth.	Stay there, Mom.		What's gotten into you?
No need.		*(JAMES exits.)*		
				Do you have rabies or something?
Really. It's no big deal.				
				Oh, this is a big deal all right. Now, you're going to go
It's over, it's It was a game. We were playing. We We were playing.		*(JAMES returns with a washcloth and gives it to SUZIE.)* Pretty rough game.		out on the balcony and you're going to take a deep breath and you're going to think about what you just did!

SUZIE:	ELIZABETH:	JAMES:	DANIEL:	MELISSA:
	I'll go out with her.			
				No, Mom! I don't want you going out there with her! I want her to be all by herself and to think about what a mean thing she did to Suzie!
	I'll go out there with her. I need to ask forgiveness for some things I've done myself.			
				No! I don't want anyone talking to her! I want her to be out there all by herself and to think about what she's done! After that I want her to apologize!

SUZIE:	**ELIZABETH:**	**JAMES:**	**DANIEL:**	**MELISSA:**
She's been punished enough already. She doesn't need to apologize.				And on her knees! She is not going to get away with this! Oh believe me! She needs to apologize!

3

The stage rotates from the dining room to the balcony. OLIVIA *comes out of the dining room, head down, followed by the others. As they walk through the living room, we see the half-empty bookcase and open cardboard boxes on the floor.*

4

On the balcony. ELIZABETH, JAMES, DANIEL, SUZIE, *and* MELISSA *are in a circle around* OLIVIA, *who is on her knees.* TYLER *films* OLIVIA *with his phone.*

MELISSA: Tyler, are you recording?

TYLER: Yeah.

A close-up of OLIVIA*'s face appears on a wall.*

MELISSA: Olivia, what do you say?

Pause.

Olivia.

OLIVIA: I'm sorry.

MELISSA: I'm sorry who?

OLIVIA: I'm sorry, Suzie.

MELISSA: And I'm sorry for?

OLIVIA: For biting you.

MELISSA: The whole sentence.

OLIVIA: I'm sorry for biting you, Suzie.

MELISSA: Into the camera.

OLIVIA: *(into camera)* I'm sorry for biting you, Suzie.

MELISSA: Suzie, do you accept her apology?

SUZIE: Yes, but only if she gets up! She's going to make me cry like that.

MELISSA: Okay, you can get up now.

OLIVIA stands up.

Now remember we have witnesses and a video. I hope you've learned your lesson. We, not one of us here, are going to tolerate big girls biting people. Now come and help us. We're going to pack the books.

Everyone goes into the apartment and disappears into the living room except ELIZABETH. On the outside wall we see OLIVIA's face as she continues to look into the camera. ELIZABETH takes out a pack of cigarettes and lights one. She smokes while the conversation continues in the living room.

SUZIE:	JAMES:	DANIEL:	MELISSA:
			Jane Eyre. I remember I wrote a sixty-page essay

SUZIE:	**JAMES:**	**DANIEL:**	**MELISSA:**
			on it for my literature class. I was so into this book!
	The National Dream by Pierre Berton. I forgot he wrote books.		
		That was before TV got him.	
	What dream's he talking about?		
			Who knows.
Why do all Canadian writers have to be such downers?			
	The Collected Poems of Irving Layton. Ma, you want to keep this?		
			God, that's so boring. Toss it in here, will you.
The Trial of Steven Truscott.			
			I've got *The Steven Truscott Story*.
	Me too!		
Sounds like your mother had a thing for Steven Truscott.			

SUZIE:	JAMES:	DANIEL:	MELISSA:
		It was one of the biggest trials Canada's ever seen.	
			What did he do again?
		He was accused of raping and murdering his classmate, Cheryl Lynne Harper. He was fourteen, she was twelve.	
I never heard about it.			
		The trial was in 1959.	
Oh okay it was a long time ago.			
		He was tried as an adult and sentenced to death by hanging. But after ten years on death row, the federal cabinet changed his sentence. A lot	
		of the evidence	Why?
	People probably didn't feel so good about hanging a kid.	was circumstantial—the police actually gave him LSD hoping he'd confess—and	

SUZIE:	JAMES:	DANIEL:	MELISSA:
		they cherry-picked witness testimony to make their case. Truscott was the last person to see Cheryl alive and his family was new to the area. He was an outsider. The perfect scapegoat.	
	Didn't he get paroled?		
		Only after ten more years in jail and several failed appeals. And then he disappeared for thirty years, until a CBC journalist decided to look into his case. After that Innocence Canada finally got him acquitted.	
			You're such a know-it-all.
	He read all the books.		
		It was a really big deal.	

OLIVIA: So did they ever catch who did it?

SUZIE:	JAMES:	DANIEL:	MELISSA:
		No.	
			So how do they know he wasn't guilty?
		When they reopened his trial in 2006, there was all kinds of fresh evidence. Turns out that Cheryl Lynne	
Okay, that's it. I give up		Harper died five hours after Truscott gave her a lift on his bike. He couldn't have killed her. Even Michael Bryant,	
	The guy that killed the bike courier?	the attorney general at the time—yeah—he apologized on behalf of the government. But Lynne Harper's family still believes he might be guilty.	
What's the point of all these trials, books, and appeals if you're still not going to			

SUZIE:	**JAMES:**	**DANIEL:**	**MELISSA:**
know who actually did it?			
	Didn't some retired OPP cop recently say this travelling salesman did it?		
		That was just a rumour.	
			That doesn't tell me if we're keeping the books or not
	Not two copies of the same book, anyway. Mom, *The Steven Truscott Story*, you want to keep it, yes or no?		
	Mom?		
			Ma?

ELIZABETH doesn't answer. Blackout on the balcony. On the outside wall, OLIVIA stares off into the darkness, as if a monster is about to jump out. She closes her eyes. Blackout.

Olivier Choinière is a playwright and director based in Montréal. He is the artistic and co-executive director of L'ACTIVITÉ. In his work, he explores different forms of representation, whether on stage or off, and seeks to give an active role to the spectator. He was the recipient of the prestigious Siminovitch Prizein 2014. A graduate in playwriting from the National Theatre School, Olivier won their Gascon-Thomas Award in 2015. His play *Ennemi public* won the Prix Michel-Tremblay in 2015 and *Manifeste de la Jeune-Fille* was honoured at the 2020 Primeurs Festival in Germany.

Bobby Theodore is a Toronto-based screenwriter, playwright, dramaturg, and translator. After graduating from the National Theatre School of Canada's playwriting section in 1998, he was a finalist for the Governor General's Literary Award in 2000 for his translation of *15 Seconds* by François Archambault. Since then, Bobby has gone on to translate over twenty-five plays from French to English. His most recent translations include *The Just* by Albert Camus and *The Law of Gravity* by Olivier Sylvestre.

First edition: September 2022
Printed and bound in Canada by Rapido Books, Montreal

Jacket design by Patrick Gray
Author photo © Charles Lafrance
Translator photo © Keith Barker

PLAYWRIGHTS
CANADA PRESS

202-269 Richmond St. W.
Toronto, ON
M5V 1X1

416.703.0013
info@playwrightscanada.com
www.playwrightscanada.com
@playcanpress